Ignatii N. Potapenko

A Russian Priest

Ignatii N. Potapenko
A Russian Priest
ISBN/EAN: 9783337242404

Printed in Europe, USA, Canada, Australia, Japan

Cover: Foto ©ninafisch / pixelio.de

More available books at **www.hansebooks.com**

A RUSSIAN PRIEST

PSEUDONYM LIBRARY

THE PSEUDONYM LIBRARY.

Paper, 1/6; *cloth*, 2/-.

1. **MLLE. IXE.** By LANOE FALCONER. 6th ed.

2. **STORY OF ELEANOR LAMBERT.** By MAGDALEN BROOKE.

3. **MYSTERY OF THE CAMPAGNA.** By VON DEGEN. 2nd ed.

4. **THE SCHOOL OF ART.** By ISABEL SNOW. 2nd ed.

5. **AMARYLLIS.** By ΓΕΩΡΓΙΟΣ ΔΡΟΣΙΝΗΣ.

6. **THE HÔTEL D'ANGLETERRE**, and Other Stories. By LANOE FALCONER.

7. **A RUSSIAN PRIEST.** By Н. ПОТАПЕНКО.

И. Н. ПОТАПЕНКО

A Russian Priest

LONDON
T. FISHER UNWIN
PATERNOSTER SQUARE
—
M DCCC XCI

PREFACE.

THIS little story of Russian life which appeared about a year ago in the *Viéstnik Evropi*, the leading Russian literary magazine, may prove interesting to those who follow the progress of events in Russia at the present day, throwing as it does, a certain amount of light upon the habits and condition of the peasants, who form the great mass of the nation, and the influence the clergy have on them. Up to this time the clergy may be said to have formed an hereditary profession, having very little in common with other classes of society, and even at the present day it often happens that when a country priest dies or retires, his place is taken by the husband of his eldest daughter. Before the liberation of the serfs in 1861, the clergy looked chiefly to the landowners for assistance and support, but since that time, the whole conditions of life in the country have completely altered, and the clergy now depend for their maintenance on the money which they receive from their parishioners for the various services and ceremonies performed. In addition to this, they always have a small quantity of church land. In some parts of the empire the peasants have fallen into a state bordering on destitution since the liberation, the landowners also are nearly ruined, and in such districts the priest scarcely earns enough to keep alive. The town clergy, on the other hand, speaking generally, may be said to be very prosperous. In a large town parish inhabited by relatively wealthy people, the system of receiving payment from every parishioner for baptisms, marriages, funerals, &c., besides two or three visits a year to each house (which have to be remunerated by a sum depending on the social position of the householder), produces a very large income. Several parishes in Moscow and Petersburg yield considerably over a thousand pounds a year in our money. Proposals which have been made from time to time to substitute a regular salary for the system of direct payments by the parishioners, have been strenuously opposed by the town clergy as prejudicial to their interests; but there can be little doubt that some such arrangement would much improve the relations between the peasants and their clergy, and it seems probable that the government will shortly introduce some change in this system, being anxious to improve and strengthen the position of the clergy, and to make them take a more important part than hitherto in primary education.

The Russian clergy are educated at the Seminary, and those who show special ability, afterwards enter the Academy, which occupies in clerical education, the same place as the University in civil education. Among the Academy professors are some of the ablest men in the empire, and to pass out of this institution with the degree of "Magistrant" implies a very high standard of learning. Such a student, from a professional point of view, is a "made man." There are several courses open to him. He may either enter the ranks of the "white" or secular clergy, get married and receive a nomination to some lucrative town living, or else he may remain a layman and become a Seminary professor; or, if he is of an ambitious disposition, he may enter the black or monastic clergy, in which case he will remain celibate, and live in the monastery in the hopes of eventually receiving an appointment as "archierèï" or bishop, the latter being always appointed from the monastic clergy.

The hero of this story, in renouncing such brilliant prospects, and preferring the poverty and hardships of the country priest's life, seems to be under the influence of the wide-spread movement of which one reads so much in the Russian literature of to-day, in the writings of Tolstoi and others, and the object of which is to enlighten and civilize the peasants. With this motive, many educated people have established so-called "intelligent colonies," that is to say, a certain number of people who have received good education, either from an inability to get government appointments, or perhaps purely from a desire to exercise a good influence on the peasants, go to the country and settle down to live as peasants, *à la Tolstoï*. Judging from recent accounts which have appeared of such enterprises, one can scarcely suppose they have been very successful. Young men and women of this class, educated as they have been in big towns, are physically incapable of carrying out their self-imposed task. Their idealistic tendencies only rouse the derision and contempt of the peasants, and the enterprise is frequently put an end to by the governor of the province, who gives them notice to leave, as their opinions and their influence on the peasants are not of a nature to please the government authorities.

There are other instances of landowners voluntarily giving up all their property to the peasants, and living on a few acres of land which they cultivate with their own hands. There have been several cases recently of people in good society in Russia giving up their appointments in the army or civil service and going into the Church with philanthropic objects. Such cases, it is true, are very rare, but it is quite a new thing for people occupying social positions of any importance to enter the Church in Russia.

The majority of those in Russia who "go to the people," as it is called, are actuated by political tendencies, and are therefore looked upon by the government with great suspicion. These reformers see that progress of liberal principles in Russia can never take place until the inertia of the great mass of the people—the peasants—be removed, and they hope by their personal influence to succeed in doing this. The government very naturally looks with distrust and suspicion on the influence which such political idealists, imbued, as they often are, with revolutionary and freethinking notions, have on the absolutely ignorant peasants, who, after hundreds of years of serfdom, obtained their freedom only thirty years ago, and who up to this time, from ignorance of how to use their newly-gained liberty, cannot be said to have improved their material welfare in any way, and in many cases are in a far worse position than in 1861.

The government of Alexander III., with the view of improving the state of things, has recently abolished the institution of "justice of the peace" in the country districts, which was introduced at the time of the emancipation, by Alexander II. They have substituted for this, the "Zemski Natchálnik," an official who has far more arbitrary and summary powers. The latter is nominated by the governor of the province and by the *maréchal de noblesse*, from the local nobility, with the design of improving the position of the nobles in the country districts, and it is hoped that this measure, in conjunction with the elementary education which is beginning to extend itself among the peasantry, and which is to be far more in the hands of the clergy than has hitherto been the case, will give the development of the peasantry a more favourable turn.

It is scarcely necessary to add that Cyril, filled as he is with philanthropic ideas of a somewhat idealistic nature, is quite free from any political tendencies. He certainly presents a striking contrast to many of his colleagues, who appear to be actuated by motives of a very different nature.

W. GAUSSEN,
Editor and Translator.

June, 1891.

A RUSSIAN PRIEST.

I.

WO individuals were prominent among the crowd which filled the barn-like waiting-room of the railway station in a provincial town in Russia. They both belonged to the clerical profession, and were attired in long cassocks. But here the resemblance between them ended, and a more attentive study of them showed clearly that they were people occupying totally different positions.

One, who stood opposite an advertisement board, carefully studying the time-table of the South-Western Railway, evidently belonged to the *élite* of the clergy in the government town. He wore a dark-green satin cassock, and on his breast hung a large cross attached to a massive chain. His full, pallid cheeks were fringed by a growth of greyish hair, which grew thicker lower down and formed a broad carefully combed beard. He wore black gloves, and on his head was a dark-grey, soft beaver hat. From time to time he pulled out a large gold watch from under his cassock, and it was evident that he f...bored at being kept waiting so long.

The other was seated on a bench in a corner of the room, in uncomfortably close proximity to a huge bundle and its fat proprietor. The first thing that struck one about him, was his very long grey beard, which, as his head was bent down, looked even longer than it really was, and seemed to reach almost to his knees. His hands, which were long-fingered and showed prominent blue veins, lay on his knees. Underneath his grey, worn-out cassock appeared large boots of coarse Russian leather. The old man was tall and thin and stooped very much. His eyes were closed and he was dozing, and his pale face had almost a death-like air. Every now and then a noise on the platform aroused him, and he gazed with a perplexed air at the crowd around him, and at the scene, evidently unfamiliar to him, and then, as if suddenly remembering the circumstances which had brought him there, dozed off again.

The clerical gentleman in the satin cassock, grew tired of studying the time-table, and choosing a moment when the other opened his eyes, went up to him. The latter jumped up immediately and straightened himself up as much as possible.

"Ah! an acquaintance, I think . . . but I can't remember where I had the pleasure of seeing you," said the priest in the satin attire, with a pleasant baritone voice with somewhat of a drawl.

"I only just this minute noticed you, father rector; allow me to recall to your recollection the deacon of the village of Ustimiévka, Ignátii Obnovliénski."

The rector assumed a mixed expression of pleasure and surprise.

"Obnovliénski! ... Obnovliénski! Yes, yes, to be sure! So you are the father of Cyril Obnovliénski? Very glad to meet you. A first-rate pupil he was; you know that we received the thanks of the academy for him.... What is he doing now? Has he finished the course at the academy?"

The deacon Obnovliénski was evidently delighted by the praise bestowed on his son by such an important personage as the rector of the seminary. His large eyes sparkled with satisfaction—indeed he used nearly to weep with transport when his younger son, Cyril, was mentioned in a flattering way by any one.

"Yes, your Reverence, he has finished; he came out first in the examination for 'Magistrant.'[1] ... Yes, first!"

"Oh! I suppose, under those circumstances, he will stay on at the academy? They always give the first one an appointment there."

"No, he is leaving," and the deacon's voice slightly trembled and became low. The old man was agitated. "Yes, certainly they always keep the first in the examination, but Cyril will not stay on; he wrote to me, 'I shall come back to you, and not leave you again,' so I suppose he will not stay on."

"H'm! ... That's strange!" said the father rector. "I confess I never heard of such a thing before."

The deacon's voice trembled slightly:

---

[1] M.A.

his heart shrank with some vague evil presentiment, and confusion before the rector, that his son, for whom the seminary had received thanks, had failed to fully justify their expectations.

"I don't understand it, either!" said he, almost in a whisper; something seemed to stick in his throat and prevent him from speaking.

"I am expecting my nephew—also from the academy. He went there at the same time as your Cyril: he has received an appointment in our seminary," said the father rector, as though wishing to change what was evidently an unpleasant subject of conversation for the other. But the deacon was no longer listening to him. The sound of the approaching train was heard, and he was hurrying to the door where the public, anxious to meet their friends, were crowding. A minute later he was standing on the platform anxiously following with his eyes the approaching train. He attentively watched it in the hope that he might see in the distance that much-loved face out of one of the windows—but, as can be imagined, he did not see anything.

The train drew up with a solemn groan under the high glass roof of the station. The deacon stood there with a confused expression watching the passengers getting out of the train. Everything seemed strange and confused to him; it appeared to him as though this bustling scene of passengers, hurrying with parcels and bags, snatches of conversation, greetings and kisses, was nothing more than a dream. A little way off he saw the rector embracing a young man with a travelling bag slung over his shoulders, and then shake hands with another young man, tall and pale, with longish light hair appearing from under his hat, and small moustaches and a clipped beard. They approached him now, the tall young man almost ran. The deacon's head swam, his legs trembled, and he hardly knew what he was doing. He embraced Cyril as though this was a parting and not an arrival. Cyril drew himself away.

"That's right, let us have one more kiss," said he, in a strong bass voice. "We must look after the luggage."

The old man followed him; at length they found the trunk, and started off in a droshky.

Cyril asked—"And is Mura[1] well?"

"Mária Gavrílovna? Yes, thank God, she is waiting for you."

"Why didn't she come to meet me?"

"She wanted to, very much. But her mother, Anna Nikoláevna, would not allow her to come—she thought it wasn't proper."

"Well, and my mother and sister and brother Nazar—are all of them well?"

"They send their love. Nazar wants to be made a priest, but the bishop refused; he said he must serve longer."

The deacon thought to himself that it was not right that his son asked after Mura first and then after his mother.

"Where do you want to go to?" asked the driver, whom, meanwhile, he had forgotten to tell.

"To the cathedral house," said the deacon, hastily; and then, turning to his son, he added, "We will go first to

---

[1] Familiar name for Mária.

Father Gávriil; I left my horses there. ... We will have something to eat and then go on to Ustimiévka, and be home by evening."

"No, no, that won't do! we must spend the night here. I have got to call on the bishop."

The old man wanted to ask why, but he refrained, and in the meanwhile unpleasant thoughts were passing in his head: "What does he want to go to the bishop for, if he has come out first in the examination? ordinary individuals go to him with requests to be made priests or even deacons. ... But the 'first magistrant.' ... What does it mean?" But a feeling of joy filled him that his beloved son had returned and was sitting by his side in the droshky, and the old man was silent and reserved his questions for another occasion. The son had no idea of these misgivings, he looked around him wondering at the various changes effected in the government town in the past two years. They were building a new church, and had paved the street leading to the station, and several new houses had sprung up.

"They are improving our town," said he, aloud, "and they have redecorated the cathedral house."

The two-storied cathedral house, at which they had arrived, was painted a dark-brown colour. Nearby, in a spacious square, stood the large but clumsy and angular edifice of the cathedral, surrounded by green railings. They paid the driver, entered the house, and ascended to the second story.

Father Gávriil Fortificantof lived in a very nice set of rooms in the cathedral house. He held the rank of third priest, and as the residents of the government town were distinguished for their generosity in good works, he enjoyed a very comfortable income. The guests ascended the narrow wooden staircase, passed through a broad glass-covered corridor and entered Father Gávriil's room. As they approached they noticed a certain amount of movement, of a quiet and sedate nature, was going on in the room. Father Gávriil himself met them. He first gave Cyril his benediction, and then embraced him three times. At that moment a solid-looking lady, Anna Nikoláevna, appeared from the drawing-room attired in a light blue morning-gown, with a cap on her head. She also kissed Cyril. In this house they called him "thou" and treated him like a son. He had been engaged to Mária Gavrilovna ever since he had been a pupil at the seminary. It need hardly be said that such an alliance, with the son of a poor village deacon, was only approved of by the parents in consideration of Cyril's peculiar aptitude for learning, and at the time it was a certainty that he would be able to pass the examination and enter the academy.

They sat down. The conversation turned upon the details of the journey and the latest town gossip. It was eleven o'clock; the lady of the house ordered *déjeuner* to be served.

"And where is Mura?" asked Cyril; "Mária Gavrilovna?" he added, correcting himself, remembering that before the parents he ought to call her so still.

"She is dressing," answered Anna Nikoláevna. But as a matter of fact Mura was long ago dressed. Her mother had kept her out of the way, considering that a young lady ought not to appear in a hurry to meet the man to to whom she was engaged, although they had not met for two years.

"When will Father Gávriil begin to cross-question him?" thought the deacon to himself, with anxiety. He very much feared this interrogation, and had not resolved to open the subject himself. He was a little afraid of his son, and recognized his inferior position of deacon, in comparison with his son's position.

Mária Gavrilovna entered the dining-room. She greeted Cyril in a friendly way, but decorously and constrainedly. She had a very commonplace oval face, with full rosy cheeks and lively brown eyes. Thick tresses of black hair carefully combed out, fell to her waist. Evidently her restrained manner was not natural. She blushed and was silent from emotion. She would have liked to embrace her *fiancé*, whose arrival she had been awaiting so impatiently, and with whom she was evidently charmed.

"Well, Cyril Ignatievitch," said Father Gávriil, "so you are first 'magistrant' in the theological academy, and gold medalist! I congratulate you." He said this in a solemn tone, but at the same time with a slight shade of levity.

The deacon's heart failed him. "The explanation is coming," thought he, and, in consequence of his agitation, he began to eat with increased appetite.

Mura gazed steadily at her newly-arrived *fiancé*, and thought to herself, "How learned he must be now!"

"Yes, quite a swell," jokingly answered Cyril.

"Certainly! And what a future you have before you."

"Now it's coming," thought the deacon.

Cyril was silent at this, but Father Gávriil was determined to clear up the mystery and began—

"But how is it you have no appointment? Have you got anything special in view?"

"Nothing whatever, Father Gávriil."

"It's a very extraordinary thing! With the gold medal too! ... I never heard of such a thing! ... Didn't they offer you anything? ... Extraordinary!"

"Yes; they offered me an appointment in the academy, but I refused it."

At these words the whole company put down their knives and forks on the table.

"Ah! that's it!" muttered the deacon, and then became afraid, feeling that he ought not to have said this.

"An appointment in the theological academy, and you refused? You must have lost your senses!" exclaimed Father Gávriil.

"It's madness!" exclaimed Anna Nikoláevna.

Mura said nothing, but felt a deep pang of regret. To live in a big city was the dream of her life.

"What could I do? I love you all; I love the warm south, the country, my birthplace, the moujiks,"[1] said Cyril, seriously and thoughtfully; "so I have come back to you," added he.

All looked at each other, and Father Gávriil said—

"Love for one's native country and relations is praiseworthy, is sublime. But why refuse that which your talent and labour has gained for you? You could come to us, see us, and return. But to refuse a professorship! and in the theological academy! It's simply a crime."

"Yes, it's wicked!" echoed Anna Nikoláevna, with a solemn expression—"it's wicked!"

"And, besides, in any case you won't live in the country," continued Father Gávriil.

"Yes, I shall," firmly and slowly said Cyril; "I am going to be a village priest."

These words had the effect of a trumpet-blast on the audience. For the first minute no one said anything. "He must be joking," thought each of them, and they looked at him. Cyril sat there serious, resolute, and pale. There was a look of firm resolution on his face. All saw at once he was not joking. Father Gávriil reddened, got up from his seat, pushing the chair away hastily, and said—

"And have you come here to make sport of us?"

"I? To make sport of you?" said Cyril, with a distressed air.

Anna Nikoláevna quickly got up from her seat, and, with the expression of one who is insulted, said—

---

[1] Peasants.

"My daughter will not marry a country priest!" and then, turning to Mária Gavrilovna, said—

"Mária, leave the room!"

Cyril also got up, and went to the window, and stood there in an evidently agitated frame of mind. He looked at his *fiancée* furtively, expecting that she would go. Mura obeyed. She felt that she was going to weep, and, feeling ashamed of herself, hurriedly turned to the door and quickly went out. Her mother followed her. Father Gávriil sat there with a red face and knitted brows. It seemed as if he wished to burst into abusive language, but instead of this he wiped his mouth with the napkin, got up, crossed himself, and without even looking at Cyril and the deacon, followed his wife and daughter.

The deacon sat motionless, his head drooping and his arms hanging down. He could scarcely grasp the reality of the scene which had just passed. Detached phrases passed through his head. "How angry Father Gávriil got!—and his wife!—the first magistrant!—the gold medal!—a village priest!... O Lord, my Creator!" and he feared to lift his head, lest he should meet the glance of his son.

Cyril stood at the window some minutes, and then energetically paced up and down the room; at length, stopping behind the chair on which his father was sitting, he said, in a trembling voice—

"Well, father, we had better pack up our traps and be off."

The deacon started.

"What! Does this mean that all is ended?"

"I suppose so," said Cyril, with a bitter smile.

"And aren't you sorry, Kiroushka¹?" asked the deacon, in a soft and timid voice.

"Of course I am. My heart is broken. They plainly refused me."

"Refused!" hoarsely whispered the deacon.

What disillusion and blasted hopes were expressed in this word! There were two things which were the pride of his life—the first, his son, who had always come out first in all his examinations, and even distinguished himself in the theological academy, and received the medal; the second, the projected alliance with Father Fortificantof's family. Such a marriage was more than he, a poor obscure village deacon, could have ventured to dream of. However, the dream had nearly been accomplished; he would have been received as a relation in the house of a protopope—and now!

He got up hastily, buttoned his cassock round his neck, and said, in a tone of despair—

"Come along, my son."

They went out into the vestibule. Cyril's heart was beating fast, but he walked with a firm step; he knew that he could not have acted otherwise. All the doors into the various rooms were closed, and no sound of movement or conversation came from them. They had already reached the glass-covered

---

¹ Familiar name of Cyril.

corridor, when the deacon said in a whisper—

"We haven't even said good-bye."

"They don't wish to," hoarsely answered Cyril, and taking up his bag began to descend the staircase.

The deacon hesitated; he quietly opened the door of the kitchen, beckoned with his finger to the cook and whispered to her—

"Anéwta, if they ask after us, say we are at the Moscófski inn."

Anéwta looked at him with surprise, and after he had descended the staircase closed the door again.

The deacon harnessed his mare to a two-wheeled cart in silence, and gathered up the hay scattered on the ground of the cathedral yard. They got into the cart without saying anything, and turned out into the street. The Moscófski inn was situated on the outskirts of the town. Arriving there, Cyril remembered that fifteen years ago they used to stop there every time when his father came to fetch him from the seminary for the holidays. Their *teliéga* used to stand in the extensive yard. The numbered rooms for the reception of guests—large, dirty, and without any conveniences—remained exactly as they had been then. Cyril entered the room, flung down his portmanteau, and began to pace about from one corner to the other, and at length the deacon went to his old acquaintance, the innkeeper, and poured out to him all his troubles.

"I tell you what, father deacon," said the innkeeper, a man of florid complexion and downright manners. "You won't be offended with what I say: but there must be a screw loose in your son's head. You may be sure of it."

The deacon was offended.

"Excuse me; if only your son had such a head, you would be a lucky man," he said, somewhat maliciously.

"My son will be an innkeeper, and he has the head for it; but yours has studied too much, and his mind has got beyond the proper limits. Don't be offended, father deacon; I say it with all sympathy for you."

The deacon was completely upset, returned to his room, and asked his son—

"I suppose you will call on the bishop to-morrow?"

Cyril was sitting on a worn-out chair, and cast a simple friendly glance at his father.

"Sit down, bátoushka, and let's have a talk. I've hardly had a word with you yet," said he, in a calm voice.

The deacon hastily sat down on the bed, which creaked and groaned under him.

"What's the good of my going to the bishop now?" continued Cyril. "To be ordained, I must be married, and I don't know any young lady except Mária Gavrilovna. We have become friends, and are accustomed to each other. All my plans are upset now."

"They are, indeed," muttered the deacon.

Cyril smiled.

"No, it's not as you imagine; I know you think I have gone out of my mind."

"God be with you! I never thought of such a thing;" and then, correcting himself, "I never thought it."

"I only wish that there should be some sort of sense in my life. You, bátoushka, although worn out by poverty, are a man of sense. If no one else understands me, you ought to. From my earliest years I have lived in the country in our poor village Ustimiévka, I have seen how the moujik lives and dies in utter darkness. His ignorance, father, is caused by poverty, and his poverty, by ignorance. Thus one engenders the other. I have loved them from my childhood for their very poverty, although I was thoughtless then and my love was not roused. But now I have learnt and read books and conversed with learned people, and my mind is awakened. I have understood that to live thoughtlessly is unworthy of the human mind. I have adopted the maxim that if a man has received enlightenment, his duty is to enlighten his neighbour. Then only, will his life leave good results behind it. And where is a more worthy object for my labours than the ignorant peasant? Light is wanted in the darkest places, bátoushka, and you know yourself how dark it is there, and therefore I decline the fine offers of a career which have been made to me, and shall devote my life to the labours of a village priest. And now, father, tell me whether you think me mad or not."

The deacon sat there with his head cast down. At length had come this explanation so long waited for, and every word of this small speech sank into his soul. He did not fully grasp his son's meaning, but felt that in these words was something right and good.

And glad he was that his son had such a right judgment; but sorry that his dreams of future advantage were ended, and that he had for an instant suspected his son of madness. All these various thoughts passed through his mind and he was silent.

Cyril got up and approached him.

"Well, bátoushka, do you approve or not?"

The deacon suddenly seized him with both hands, and said, in a trembling voice—

"You are a good fellow, your idea is in accordance with the gospel—in accordance with the gospel."

Cyril kissed his grey head, and his face was lit up with a joyful smile.

"Well, bátoushka, at any rate you understand me! It is easier to live, feeling that some one, at least understands one. I know that my mother and all my relations will be against me. I had already counted on your approval."

"Yes, yes; but how about Mura? . . . If you love her, are accustomed to her, this will be bitter for you."

Cyril began to walk silently up and down the room, and the deacon, so as not to interfere with his thoughts, went out. He stood some time at the doorway of the inn, and suddenly his face assumed a determined expression. He returned to the vestibule, took his hat, and started off furtively across the yard. Then he quickened his pace and almost ran back to the cathedral house.

II.

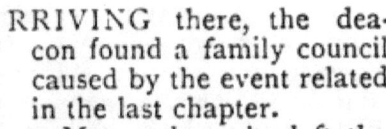RRIVING there, the deacon found a family council caused by the event related in the last chapter.

Mura, when she left the dining-room, had retired to her own room and nervously awaited the result. When her mother came in and told her that Cyril and his father had gone and that the affair was at an end, she burst into tears and declared that she would never marry any one but Cyril.

"What folly," said her mother. "You shall not not go and bury yourself in the country."

"I don't care, I love him, and will live where he does. . . . It's no use your saying anything. I shall simply run away with him, and then there will be a scandal."

Mária Gavrilovna, although usually of a retiring and mild disposition, on certain occasions showed the determination of character, which she probably inherited from her mother. On such occasions Father Gávriil used to shut himself up in his study, leaving it to the ladies to settle between themselves. And ordinary everyday matters were arranged without his interference. But this incident was of such an exceptional nature, and as Anna Nikoláevna did not feel equal to the occasion, she asked her husband to bring his influence to bear on Mura.

"Do you know what country life means, and how they live there?" said Father Gávriil. "Without a single living intelligent soul—nothing but moujiks. Deadly *ennui* and weariness. The moujiks, in whose company you will have to live, are uncivilized, ignorant, and dirty. During the winter you will be blocked up by snowstorms and blizzards, and in the summer you will be scorched."

"I don't care—I love him!" obstinately answered Mura.

Father Gávriil, as though convinced of the uselessness of his efforts, was silent for a time, trying to find a more powerful argument.

"And there's another thing you forget," said Anna Nikoláevna, in her turn. "You love him, that's right enough; but does he love you? I don't think so. Judge for yourself. When a man really loves his *fiancée* he does all in his power to make things pleasant for her. That's my opinion."

"Quite so," rejoined Father Gávriil, remembering that in his time he had fulfilled his duty in this respect.

"Yes, and see how he acts. He gets some foolish idea into his head, and in order to carry it out, he is ready to bury you alive. No, he cannot love you."

"Ah no, mátoushka,¹ he does love her—he really does!" exclaimed a fourth voice, with determination, and looking towards the door, they saw the deacon who had entered, like a ghost, unob-

¹ Name given to wives of the clergy.

served. On this occasion, he was not as usual, timid and retiring, but in his voice there was a tone of determination. He placed his right hand on his heart, and in a firm tone said—

"Father Gávriil, mátoushka, for the Lord's sake listen to me! My son said to me, 'Why go to the bishop now, when they have refused me? It's all over with me now, for I cannot marry any one else, for I don't know and don't wish to know any other woman on earth except Mura.'" [1]

The deacon wept.

Mura, hearing such a pathetic sentiment from his lips, began to sob again, and Father Gávriil and his wife cast down their heads and were silent.

"How does he explain this extraordinary course of action?" asked Anna Nikoláevna, after a short silence, without looking at him.

"He wishes to act in accordance with the gospel."

Anna Nikoláevna assumed a very dissatisfied air. "I am not aware that the gospel teaches that it is absolutely necessary to live in the country."

Father Gávriil, without answering this remark, said—

"This is my opinion: Mária is of an age to act for herself. If she loves him so much that she can decide to marry him we will agree, and to teach her husband sense afterwards will be her affair! I suppose that in time he will become sensible, and he can always exchange for a town living. But she must decide for herself."

The deacon went up to him, kissed his

---

[1] A candidate for deacon's orders must be married.

hand and forehead, and turned round to his wife and said—

"Mátoushka, will you allow me?"

"Very well. But I am not responsible for this," said she, holding out her hand, which he kissed with great impetuosity. Mura threw herself into her mother's arms and there was a pathetic scene of mutual embracings.

The deacon went back to the inn as fast as his legs could carry him, in order to bring Cyril to the Fortificantofs. But before he was formally recognized as a Mura's *fiancé*, he underwent an examination at the hands of Father Gávriil and his wife. He even promised that if experience should show him anything better he would listen to reason. After this he was allowed to see Mura.

"Mura," said he, "I ought to explain . . ."

"Don't explain, Cyril, I don't want to know anything. . . . I love you, and that's enough . . ."

And she squeezed his hand so confidingly that he did not attempt to make any further explanations. In the evening they walked together; Cyril told her about the magnificent palaces, bridges, museums, and theatres of the capital.

"It must be very nice there," remarked Mura, timidly, fearing this might be a reproach.

"Yes, but there is no life there—people don't live there, but pass time. Life is consumed by the flame of excitement and amusement; I would not live there even a year if I had my choice."

"And I could live there for an age," thought Mura to herself.

The next day Cyril got up early, as

the bishop received at eight o'clock in the morning. He dressed himself in the clumsy suit of clothes provided by the authorities for the students of the academy, drank tea, and left the protopope's house before any of its inmates had got up. The deacon, however, was already up, and went with his son to the gates of the bishop's house, and said to him—

"The bishop will treat you with respect, as you have shown yourself a learned and distinguished man. But be careful to treat him with great respect . . . and if you can manage to put in a word for your brother Nazar, do so."

Cyril found at the entrance a crowd of people, chiefly country clergy in worn-out cassocks and caftans.[1] Some of them had a complacent air: as, for instance, two fat popes who had come to get permission for an exchange of livings; others, with fear and trembling, were awaiting banishment to a monastery for some irregularity. There were also women, evidently the widows of clergy, who had come to petition for pensions or for permission to live on in the parish as caretakers of the church, where their husbands had served, maybe thirty or forty years. Cyril, in his capacity of "magistrant" of the academy, was immediately admitted into the presence of the bishop and the rest had to wait. The bishop received him in a friendly way, as the thanks which the seminary had received for Cyril, had reflected more or less credit on the bishop himself.

"I know—I know all about it. The father rector of the academy wrote to

---

[1] A long coat worn by the Russian peasants.

me. They were counting on you, and you refused them on account of illness. H'm! . . . There doesn't seem much the matter with you."

The bishop was a very old man, but was very vigorous for his age and fond of talking; his perfectly grey beard was always wagging. He was short and somewhat stout; his face was simple and good-natured, but he liked to appear stern, and to have it understood that he kept the diocese in good order. Although he had the reputation of being strict, very strict even, still there were not ten men to be found in the diocese whom he had punished. He would talk and threaten and then send the culprit home in peace. Cyril seated himself in accordance with the bishop's invitation and said—

"I am perfectly well, your Reverence. My illness was only a formal excuse for refusing the appointment offered to me."

"I don't quite understand; explain, if you please, my son."

"Well, your Reverence, this is the cause of my visit to you. I wish to explain my intentions to you. I wish to find a place as a country priest."

"What do you mean? You have finished at the academy, and received the gold medal, and wish to be a country priest?"

It was hardly surprising that the bishop was astonished. This was the first time in his life, that he had ever had such a petition made to him. As a rule, the academicians were only satisfied with the very best places, and wished to go straight to the cathedral, or, in any case, to one of the very best town churches, and then in the capacity of chief clergyman.

"I don't understand you; please explain," added the bishop, looking at him with great curiosity.

"I wish to serve the lesser brethren—those that live in darkness," thoughtfully answered Cyril.

"Oh, that's it!" said the bishop; "only I don't understand why you have thus decided."

"I don't care about town life; a large income has no attractions for me," continued Cyril. "My heart is in the village, where I was bred and born."

"This is very sensible! May God bless you!" added the bishop, in delight. "You will be an example to the others."

He got up, went to Cyril, and kissed him on the forehead.

"But what living shall I give you? I have only one or two very poor ones to give now, all the best are occupied. And you deserve the very best."

"No, no," added Cyril, hastily. "I don't want a good one. Give me a living that will support me with a family."

"God bless you!" said the bishop again, affected by the young man's disinterestedness.

He wished to do something pleasant for him, to distinguish him in some way.

"You have a brother—the deacon Nazar—tell him to call on me. I will make him a priest, and give him a good place."

Cyril bowed, and the bishop continued—

"Go; and God be with you. Choose a wife, and prepare yourself for the priesthood. I will appoint you to a living."

He blessed the young man, embraced him, and said—

"It is a pity all the same that our town will lose you. You would have been a good preacher. I remember when you were at the seminary here you distinguished yourself in preaching. Well, tell your brother to come."

Cyril left in a happy frame of mind. In the first place, he rejoiced that the bishop understood him. It was pleasant also, that his father and Nazar would both be gratified with the bishop's kindness.

The people who were waiting in the bishop's ante-room looked at him with respect and envy. All knew that he was a magistrant and the gold medalist, and thought, "Lucky fellow; he will get the best place in the diocese—and he is quite a boy, too."

In the episcopal courtyard Cyril met the rector and his nephew, Evgénii Mejof, the latter very smartly dressed. His black frock coat had evidently been made to order; it fitted well, and was made of good cloth. His hat was new, and he had black gloves. He carried himself very importantly, and was, in fact, quite a swell. The father rector was dressed in a black cassock with the regalia on his breast. At the gate stood the seminary carriage. It was evident that the rector was taking his nephew to present him to the bishop.

"Been to pay your respects?" asked Mejof, hurrying after his uncle.

"Yes," answered Cyril, shortly.

"And I have come with my uncle to

try and get the place of the inspector whom they have removed.

"He doesn't lose time," thought Cyril to himself, especially as Mejof had finished the academy course without any distinction, and it was not even sure whether he would be able to count on the degree of "magistrant."

"Yes; my uncle is using his influence. The salary is a very good one."

"I suppose so," said Cyril, absently.

"Quarters and even firing included. Not bad."

"No."

At this moment the father rector came up.

"Well, Obnovliénski, what are your plans for the future?"

Cyril did not feel inclined to tell him. He had never taken a fancy to the father rector, and detected in his character an uncandid, and even false note.

"Oh, I really don't know yet. I shall go and talk it over with my family."

"Ah, that's right. . . . Come along, Evgénii."

Cyril bowed and parted company with them.

"How easily a man succeeds who is only keen about his own interests," thought he, remembering the very limited capacities of young Mejof.

III.

IGNÁTII OBNOVLIÉNSKI started off with his son Cyril in their springless conveyance, the wheels of which gave out a peculiar squeaking sound, which could be heard for a couple of versts around. They had already been on the road five hours, and the travellers were grey with dust. The deacon was half asleep, and was every now and then aroused by an unusual jolt. Cyril was looking around him and reflections were crowding into his mind. On both sides of the wide and tortuous high road, extended fields of ripe barley. Near by, was a farmhouse surrounded by an extensive kitchen-garden. All around was silent. Every living being had sought refuge from the scorching rays of the sun.

Cyril thought to himself how all this scene was just as he had left it three years before—just as though he had only left his native home yesterday. All was grey, monotonous—no change, no movement either backward or forward.

"We are almost there now," said Cyril, glancing on the left-hand side whither the road turned.

The village came in view suddenly, with its white church, with the neglected and moss-grown garden of the squire, the pothouse, a stone building with a tile roof at the entrance to the village. On one side stood the squire's house in a half-ruined condition, although there were people who could remember the time when the inmates lived in every possible comfort.

The impression produced by the village of Ustimiévka was one of poverty, monotony, and utter *ennui*, and the traveller felt an instinctive desire to pass by it without stopping.

"Here we are at last," said the deacon, shaking himself, and urging on his beasts with the ends of the reins.

These animals, seeing how near they were to home were going faster of their own accord. They passed the public-house and reached the church. The deacon took off his hat and crossed himself.

"We have arrived, thank God!" said he, expressively. "There is our house. You will find everything as you left it."

Passing down the village street, the moujiks seeing, or rather hearing, Father Ignátii's conveyance, took off their hats, and looked to see who the stranger was sitting with the deacon, and recognizing Cyril, nodded to him. One old woman could not restrain herself, and pointing at Cyril, cried out, "Why, here's our Kiroushka arrived." Cyril took off his hat and bowed to her. He was glad that they called him by the same name that they called him fifteen years ago. At length they arrived at the deacon's house. This was nothing more than a common moujik's hut built of clay, the only difference being, that it was a little larger than the rest and better kept. They entered the half-closed gates leading to the plot of ground in front of the house. The green shutters were closed.

The door into the hut opened with a noise, and Cyril's relations appeared. He kissed a thin, wrinkled, and regular-featured woman, with a face almost as pale as his own. Her expression was stern and even repelling. This was his mother. His sister Motia, a girl of fifteen years old, looked at him with an air of curiosity, but seemed somewhat shy and confused. His young brother Mefódii, still a pupil at the seminary, tried to look grave and self-contained. It seemed to Cyril as though he was scarcely friendly with him. His old aunt, Anna Evgraphóna, from some unknown cause, wept. His relations all seemed to greet him in a more or less formal manner. Mefódii occupied himself in unharnessing the horses, and remarked that one of them had a sore back.

"Let's come into the dining-room," said the deacon's wife; "we shall get a sunstroke if we stand here. Will you be ready soon, father?"

"No, no, don't wait for me. I will come soon."

The deacon had a secret hope that the cross-examination would take place in his absence, and that he would not have to witness the first effects of the disappointment. Cyril followed his mother into the room. Motia and her aunt followed them, and quickly disappeared into another room. In the corner hung a gilt " eikon " representing the Virgin, before which a hanging lamp was burning. A long sofa with a grey canvas covering, was the chief adornment of this reception-room, used chiefly only when there was company. In the middle of the room stood a round table with a white knitted cover. On it stood a vase with artificial flowers. In a line with the wall were several varnished chairs with high backs, a cupboard with glass doors, containing crockery, and a looking-glass. The deacon's wife decorously stood in front of the "eikon" and crossed herself, then she kissed the cross which was lying on the table, and gave it to Cyril and his aunt.

"Now then, Cyril, sit down and tell us all about your plans," said she, herself sitting on one of the chairs.

He felt very agitated. His mother had asked him the one question which he least cared to answer. He was silent.

"How handsome he is—quite a picture!" said at length the aunt; and this evidently calmed her, she stopped crying. Motia stood at the doorway and looked at her brother with a coquettish half smile. Mefódii came into the room, sat down abruptly, and lit a cigarette.

"Well, you have finished with the academy?" asked the deacon's wife.

"Yes," answered Cyril.

"Well, and what next? You will be a professor, I suppose?"

"No, mother, I think not."

"Well, what? a protopope?"

"No, I shall not be a protopope."

"You don't mean to say you are going to be a monk? But it would be very nice to be a bishop. The only thing is, it is so long to wait."

"I don't advise you to go to the monastery, to shut yourself up from the world," dolefully said the aunt.

"I haven't the least idea of going to the monastery. I don't want to be a bishop."

"Well, what then?"

"I wish to live in the village, and be a country priest."

"What are you talking about? Every seminarist becomes a country priest! What was the good of your going to the academy?"

"In order to learn, mother."

"And what's the good of your learning if you bury yourself in the country? Why Father Porphirii's son finished the academy course last year, and they gave him the first place in the church of the district town."

"Yes, I know. But to tell the truth I hardly know my own plans myself. Well, and how are you all?"

Cyril said this, intending to smooth down the effects of his explanation. But it did not produce this result. They answered his questions in a perfunctory sort of way. His brother, the seminarist, looked at him suspiciously, and looked as if he would like to ask him some quibbling question, but could not make up his mind to do so. Motia, with an expression of deep disappointment, went into the next room and sat down at the window. For some time they had all of them, including the deacon himself, reckoned on Cyril's being made a professor in the seminary, and perhaps in the course of time rector. No one could understand this sudden change, and they all attributed it to some external circumstances. Cyril began to eat, and having drunk a wineglassful of *vodka*, remarked—

"This fish is very good."

"Yes, it's from the town. It can't be got here," answered the deacon's wife; and they were all silent again.

Cyril continued to eat in silence. The joyful frame of mind in which he had entered his native village had soon given way to feelings of a different nature. He did not expect such a cold welcome. He knew quite well that this was in consequence of what he had told them. If he had only told them that he was going to be a professor or protopope they would have all been perfectly happy. He knew that his mother only restrained herself because this was the first interview, but that to-morrow there would be an unpleasant scene, reproaches and tears. Cyril knew it would be utterly vain to try and explain his ideas to her. She was a woman of no culture, barely possessed the rudiments of education, and she was unable to understand such abstract ideas as devoting one's services to one's neighbour from evangelical motives.

The deacon's wife went out of the room. Cyril continued to eat, and his brother lit another cigarette. At length he said, in a confused tone, looking at the door—

"Tell me, please, Cyril, you have not passed the examination?"

Cyril smiled, and said—

"Oh, yes, I finished right enough, and if you don't believe me, look here." And he pulled out of his waistcoat pocket a thick document and handed it to his brother, who unfolded it, perused it, and threw it down on the table.

"I do not understand it! There must be some other reason. He's come out as 'magistrant' and with the gold medal. Look here, mother, and Motia! Why, even our inspector at the seminary never got his degree. No, it beats me!"

"I'll explain it to you afterwards," said Cyril, attacking some rice pudding, which he was very fond of. His mother and Motia meanwhile looked at the diploma.

"We must frame it," said Motia.

She remembered that their incumbent, Father Agaphon, had all his diplomas of priesthood and the right to wear certain vestments, &c., framed and hung in a row on the wall.

"And, notwithstanding this, nothing more!" said the deacon's wife, with a sigh.

The aunt now appeared and looked at the diploma with surprise.

"Well! Fortified yourself?" said the deacon, coming in. He cast an inquiring glance at the faces of all present and saw that it was already out. But he remembered that he had some pleasant news to impart, and said, turning to his wife, "You know, Arisha, that Cyril called on the bishop, who received him very well, and said, 'You have a brother, Nazar, who wants to be made a priest; tell him——' What do you think he said?" The deacon seeing that all were listening with great interest, stopped, so as to tease them. "Supposing I don't tell you what he said."

"Well, tell us—what did he say?"

"Aha! Curiosity! I don't think I shall tell you."

"Well, why on earth did you begin!" However, all knew that it would soon come out.

"He said, 'Tell him to come to me and I will make him a priest.'"

"Really?"

The dry and stern face of the deacon's wife lit up. It had long been the object of her ambition that Nazar should become a priest. In comparison with this, even Cyril's academical career had occupied a second place: Cyril she regarded as a big bird who would get some important appointment, perhaps a thousand versts away, and they would only know him by name for the future. Nazar, however, was a man living very near, and with a heap of children, and always was under her eye. The idea that her second son, a "magistrant," was going to be a country clergyman, very much vexed her, but, on the other hand, it was very good news that her eldest son would be made a priest, although, probably, only a country one. Mefódii joyfully rubbed his hands; Motia jumped about the room; and the aunt wept for joy.

"Is this really true?" said the deacon's wife.

"Well, I should hardly invent such a story; but if you don't believe it, ask Cyril."

They were all rejoiced at this news, and made various enraptured remarks to one another about Nazar and his wife Lunia: how glad they would be, and how they would now be able to send their eldest daughter to the diocesan school, which to this time their limited means had prevented them from doing.

"I tell you what, my dear! It's time for me to retire," said the deacon, with emotion. "It's really time—see how old I am getting."

"What do you mean?" said his wife.

"I shall put myself on the retired list, and we will go and live with my son. Mefódii will have soon finished his time at the seminary."

His wife assumed a stern expression, looked straight at him, and said—

"That will never do."

"Why? Nazar is a kind-hearted fellow."

"Every one is kind as long as you don't ask them to put their hands in their pockets; but if you do, they are like wolves."

Cyril looked at his mother's pale face and thought what a hard life she must have led to be so deeply embittered. Somehow he had never remarked this before.

"Ah, my dear," said the deacon, good-naturedly, "why do you take such a bad view of people, and not believe in any one, even in your own flesh and blood?"

"I don't believe in them," said the deacon's wife, in a decided tone.

"I believe in every one of God's creatures; it's only Christian."

"And that's why every one gets round you."

"Well, let them; I still hold my opinion."

The conversation soon turned on the bishop's kindness again. In the evening they formed a plan for telling Nazar about it. Nazar was deacon in a neighbouring village, about thirty versts off.

The following day, they harnessed the horses, and Cyril and Mefódii set out together, along the broad road extending over the steppe. The rays of the sun had scarcely dissipated the cold night air. Cyril felt an unusual flow of good spirits. He told his brother what an excellent effect the country air had on him, and how he would not exchange life there, for life in any capital.

"I can't see anything pleasant in country life : neither people nor amusement—nothing but *ennui!*" exclaimed Mefódii. "I don't understand you a bit."

"Well, if any one had said the same thing to me when I was your age I should not have understood them," answered Cyril; "I still hankered after town life, like you : it seemed to me then, as if life was only to be found there— and here, in the country, nothing but a vegetating existence. But now I have changed my opinion. Life is really only here. People here live for existence; but in the town, life is purely conditional. Everything there is done in accordance with convention, and man there, is the slave of convention. People there live for themselves, but here you can share what you have with your neighbour. For instance, town life is expensive. In order to live properly there, all one's attention must be turned to earning the necessary means. Neither time nor strength remains to be devoted to one's neighbours. And life here costs practically nothing ; you have as much time for work as you like. Here, and here only, is one master of one's time, of one's strength, of one's capabilities. Here only, can one devote one's whole attention to the service of one's fellows."

"Is this what they taught you at the academy?" asked Mefódii, very much astonished at these sentiments.

"What?"

"Why, all that you've just been saying."

"No, they don't teach these things—each one learns them by himself."

They arrived at midday; Nazar was very glad to see them, and embraced Cyril with feeling. He was sorry, however, to remark how thin he had grown.

"And you are fatter than ever," said Cyril; "it's really time for you to stop."

Nazar despairingly waved his arms. This was his great misfortune. He was incredibly fat, and even now and then got seriously alarmed about it. Nothing seemed to be of any use; he had tried violent exercise, and given up sleeping after dinner; he used to bathe, and he took every one's advice. Some one had told him that strong tea dries up the system. He began drinking black concoctions of tea day and night. He tried drinking vinegar, moderate diet, but it was all in vain. He had a fearful appetite, and ate enough for five ordinary people, and was not unsusceptible to the charms of *vodka*. He was over forty years of age; he had seven children, and his wife, Lukéria Grigoriévna, usually called in the family Lunia, gave every hope that in the course of time their number would be doubled. This small, thin, and lively little lady presented a great contrast to Nazar. In all domestic affairs, his wife was the absolute head. Nazar, however, fulfilled his duties of deacon, for the simple reason, that in this department, his wife could not take over the management of affairs. But in all other matters, owing to his corpulence, he did not interfere, and Lunia managed the household and education of the children excellently, and even baked the *pain béni* herself. She never complained about want of strength or having too much work to do. She was thoroughly practical. Nazar worshipped his wife, and was simply in love with her, and thought her beautiful, notwithstanding that there were already wrinkles on her dark face, and her hair was prematurely turning grey.

Mefódii ran into the cattle-yard, where Lunia was busy looking after a calf, and told her the joyful news. She excitedly ran out to tell her husband, intending, however, to have some sport with him.

"Well, Nazar, do you know that Cyril has seen the bishop, and the bishop told him that he wanted to speak to his brother Nazar, and that he would have to put him on the retired list?"

"Lord have mercy on us!" exclaimed Nazar, in a fright, crossing himself. "What does this mean?"

"He said that you were so fat you could not serve any longer."

But seeing the look of despair which her joke caused the credulous Nazar, Lunia burst out laughing, and told him the whole truth, which Cyril confirmed. Nazar was, of course, in indescribable ecstasy, and would have jumped with joy, if only his weight had allowed him to do such a thing.

He at once began to think about the better circumstances in which they would assuredly find themselves after his elevation to the priesthood, about spacious lodgings, about his daughter's education, and, above all things, about getting leave of absence, so as to go to Kief or Kharkoff and be treated by a doctor there to cure his corpulency.

All these visions would now be realized, thanks to that one word from the bishop. The brothers dined together, and after dinner the young people returned to Ustimiévka. Motia ran out to meet them, and got into the conveyance near the church, and told them that an unpleasant scene had occurred at home during their absence: her mother had not slept all night; two feelings had disturbed her—one of joy for Nazar's promotion, the other grief on account of Cyril's incomprehensible, voluntary abnegation of his brilliant prospects. In the morning her nerves were quite deranged. The deacon, remarking this, said that he would have to spend the morning on business with the incumbent. But she would not let him go. At first there were sighs and reproaches of a general nature. "With other people things went all right," said the deacon's wife. "Their children grew up and attained their various objects. So-and-so's son passed through the seminary and at once got a good place in the town. There was the diocesan subdeacon's son, who had only come out in the third class, had at once been appointed to the cemetery church in the town;" and other instances. "But with them, somehow, things were quite different. Their son had astonished every one by his success, come out first in the academy, and was now going to bury himself as a country priest. Every one would point at them with scorn, and say that all the academy and fine learning was of no use. And Cyril's father, instead of showing him his folly and putting him in the right path, had actually encouraged him. Evidently God was punishing them for their sins," &c. Then her tears began to come. The aunt, of course, also wept in a quiet sort of way, and had hidden herself in the lumber room, and finally the deacon's wife had taken to her bed.

"See what my children have brought me to!" and then more tears.

Cyril sat on the bed and took her hand in his, and said, in his kind voice—

"You are not well, mother. If you would only listen to me quietly I would explain this to you."

"How can you explain?" she cried, tragically.

"I will tell you about my determinations, mother. You are vexed with me for having refused a good place, and because I had decided to be a country priest. Judge for yourself, mother. We have always been poor together. You have worked hard all your life, and hard work has worn you out. Poverty and labour, mother, these are our inheritance, and these have made us dear to one another. I wish to be of service to those near and dear to me. I don't care to serve the rich, but the poor. I wish to live thus, as you have lived. I feel the greatest respect to you for your hard-working life, and wish to live in a similar way. I have learned this from you. You planted the seed of this idea in my breast, and I have cultivated it."

It is hard to say how these words affected the deacon's wife. These arguments scarcely had any effect on her discontented mind. But the kind voice of her son, his loving glance, had a soothing effect on her. The hard expression of discontent and bad humour left her face, and she quietly drew Cyril to her and kissed him.

"Ah! Cyril," said she, in a quiet voice, "how I had counted on you—how I had hoped! I had hoped for the elevation of our family in the world."

"Oh, that will be! Only wait. Let me first satisfy the longings of my heart."

Cyril remained with her for half an hour. The deacon, hearing this conversation from the next room, wondered at his son's art in so quickly calming the storm—an art which, after many years of fruitless effort, he had never achieved, notwithstanding his extreme submission to his wife. Cyril's mother soon got up again and went about the ordinary affairs of life. And the subject was not broached again.

Nazar, on his way to the town, stopped with his relations, and received the solemn benediction of his parents. His mother gave him a lecture as if he was a child, to which the good-natured Nazar listened with all humility and seriousness. In fact, he was nothing more than a child, and, starting on such a serious business without Lunia, felt the ground under his feet somewhat insecure. The affair stood thus—that if the bishop had not changed his mind, he would have to live alone in the town at some inn for not less than a week, and this appeared to him quite an exploit.

In the deacon's house the days following Nazar's departure, all were in a state of anxiety as to his fate. Cyril alone was perfectly calm, because he knew the bishop had promised this seriously, and would keep his word. The deacon could not believe in such good fortune until it was an accomplished fact. His wife took a pessimist view, and was persuaded the thing would hang fire somehow; but after two days they began to think, that if it had turned out badly, Nazar would have already returned, and as he was still in the town it must mean that he was preparing for the priesthood.

"But maybe that he is doing penance," said the deacon's wife, although she was more inclined now to take the general and favourable view of the case.

Sunday arrived. The deacon arrayed himself in his best cassock, oiled and smoothed his hair, and wore a happy and contented expression.

"It's a certainty now that the bishop will lay his hands on him to-day," said he, with a triumphant smile, and during mass, he read the liturgy with especial emphasis and pronounced the words in an intoning voice. Every hour his agitation increased. After church, he could not eat anything at dinner. As one who had always been, and would always be, a deacon, he looked upon the priesthood, as an almost unattainable dignity, and suddenly Nazar, who seemed just such another as himself, one destined to lifelong service as a deacon, had to-day taken this important step up the ladder of life. His wife, too, was much agitated, but she tried to hide her feelings, and kept asserting, that she still did not believe in Nazar's preferment.

At length, in the evening, Nazar himself arrived. He entered the room with an expression of radiant solemnity, and stopping at the doorway attentively and reverently made the sign of the cross, and bowed towards the sacred image, and then turning to the family, who were sitting drinking tea, he silently blessed them. All understood that his consecration to the priesthood had taken place, got up from their seats and also silently crossed themselves. Although their joy was great, they were silent at first. Each in turn received the benediction of the new priest. Then they began to ask Nazar all about it. He told his whole story to the minutest details, and when he came to his first interview with the bishop, turning to Cyril, he said—

"He spoke of you in the most gratifying terms: he said you were an example for the whole diocese, and that it was really on account of your Christian humility that he consented to make me a priest; he also told me to say that he had got a place for you, and that you are to marry quickly, and come to him."

The whole family except the deacon looked with intense perplexity at Cyril.

Nazar passed the night at Ustimiévka, and Cyril went to the town on the following day.

IV.

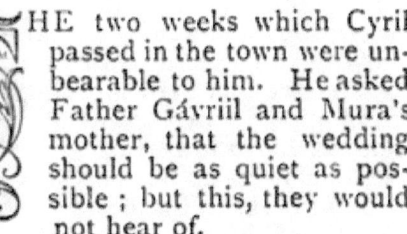HE two weeks which Cyril passed in the town were unbearable to him. He asked Father Gávriil and Mura's mother, that the wedding should be as quiet as possible; but this, they would not hear of.

"We have already given in to you too much. But about this matter, we are going to have our own way!" said Mura's mother; and, at the recollection of these concessions, she heaved a deep sigh. Mura also expressed a wish that on the evening of the wedding, there should be a reception in her father's house. She openly admitted to Cyril, that this had long been her dream; and Father Gávriil said that his position in the town made this a matter of necessity, so that further objections were perfectly useless.

And so, on the appointed evening, the second floor of the cathedral house was brilliantly illuminated, and in the cathedral the large chandelier was lit, the episcopal choir sang, and the archdeacon of the cathedral himself read the Epistle. The whole of the clerical society of the town was present, all the marriageable ladies, also on the lookout for eligible husbands—academicians if possible—with their fat mammas, seminary professors, some of the pupils in the upper classes, all helped to make a substantial congregation in church during the ceremony, and afterwards adjourned to the cathedral house and made merry there till morning. Mura was happy and lively, and looked very pretty in her snow-white attire with a mass of flowers on her head. Cyril felt uncomfortable in his dress-clothes, but they suited him, in his character of academician—a character which presupposes a deal of learning and seriousness.

Mefódii and Motia were the only ones of his relations present. The old people were afraid of the brilliancy, and said, "We should be out of place there." Lunia could not leave her children, and Nazar excused himself on account of his fatness; and besides, at this time he was making a move to the place where he had been appointed incumbent.

Two days after the wedding, Cyril called on the bishop. "Ah!" said the bishop, greeting him in a friendly way, "I know all about it; Father Gávriil has told me. You have got a nice girl for a wife. Well, I have got an appointment for you. It will not be far from your parents: Lúgovoë. Do you know it?"

"Lúgovoë?"

"Well, aren't you satisfied?"

"There are two other clergymen there, your Reverence."

"Well, and you will be their chief."

"I am afraid of this. How shall we get on together?"

"What nonsense; and with your good-nature, too! No, don't make any objections to this; I have decided it, and it shall be. It's not a bad village—it's got a bazaar, a school, and a post office. It's not like being completely buried. So prepare yourself. Friday is a *fête* day, and I will ordain you deacon, and on Sunday—a priest. Go, and God be with you."

Cyril raised no more objections. But still, the appointment did not at all satisfy him. This village Lúgovoë extended over a very large space and contained a large number of parishioners. He was not afraid of that. But he would not be alone. His colleagues would be sure to oppose his ideas. He did not even reckon on the possibility of finding in them, sympathizers or helpers. There would be, he thought, disagreements, quarrels, and all sorts of unpleasantnesses. But still, he could not make up his mind to object to the bishop's decision, after all he had done for him, and the kind sympathy he had shown him in this matter. He said to himself, "I must take my chance. In any case I shall stick to my own line. No one shall induce me to leave the path I have marked out for myself. And who knows?—maybe all is for the best."

About this time he began to experience a constant agitation. All that up to this time had existed in his mind in theory, would now take a practical form. Practical life was rapidly approaching, and he would have to be prepared for it. Sometimes when sitting beside Mura, he would take her hand and say,

"Ah, Mura! it's a difficult problem, how to find sufficient strength for the struggle."

Mura had the very haziest notion of the nature of these problems, but she did not at all like his talking in that strain. These doubts, however, rapidly passed away, and he explained to himself that they were merely caused by a deranged state of nerves, and that he had no grounds for doubting his strength.

"We are still so young, Mura! When we get old we shall begin to doubt our strength."

Mura agreed to this also, as she did to almost everything he said. She loved him for his youth, his wisdom, his sympathy, his earnestness, but considered his ideas altogether beyond her reach.

On Friday, Cyril came home from church in clerical garb. When Mura saw him in this costume she almost fainted, but recovering herself, began to cry.

"What's the matter with you?" asked Cyril, trying in vain to console her.

Cyril seemed strange to her in this dress. She was accustomed to see him in ordinary clothes, like other young men, and all of a sudden, these had vanished under a broad, long cassock—under that costume which drove away all ideas of love and romance. Of course she had known that this change would come about, but when it actually occurred, and he stood before her—a clergyman, without the least chance of his ever being like any ordinary young man again, as she had loved him, her heart involuntarily sank within her and she could not resist crying.

"But look here, Mura! I am just the same as I was before; I have not changed because my clothes are different!"

"How strange and ridiculous you look!" exclaimed Mura, almost smiling in spite of her tears. He looked in the glass, and could not help laughing at himself. Certainly he did look strange. His short hair, cut yesterday "for the last time"; his clean-shaven chin and lips—also "for the last time"; his young face and thin figure: all this gave him the air of a man who had "got himself up" for a joke, the clerical garments being almost invariably accompanied by long hair and beard, and a corpulent figure. But this was no joke, and Mura knew it. Hence her tears.

His mother-in-law congratulated him, at the same time looking at his costume in a somewhat sarcastic way. Her tenderest feelings were offended. The secret ambition of all priests' wives is to get their daughters married in the secular world. She had counted on her son-in-law becoming an inspector in the seminary, after his brilliant achievements, or else perhaps a professor in some academy; and then, when he reached middle age, that he would be ordained and get some post as protopope straight off. But now she had given her consent she felt she must make the best of a bad job, and hence her dry congratulation on this occasion without a word more.

Father Gávriil, who had assisted at Cyril's ordination, took things more calmly; he knew that the bishop approved of Cyril's action, and secretly hoped that this would help his career afterwards. He would soon get tired of the country, his foolish notions would pass off, and then the bishop would give him the best place in the town at once.

On Sunday Cyril was ordained priest. Various thoughts and feelings passed through his mind during those few minutes when the ceremony was going on. At length came the moment, when he formally, and publicly took upon himself that duty, the fulfilment of which, constituted for him the whole aims and interests of his life. At this moment he felt a secret self-satisfaction. He knew many people who talked a great deal about the responsibilities of life, but who were lacking in resolution to carry their words into action. And all his life he had talked about this duty, and had as yet, got no further. He was now leaving words behind him, and had marked out for himself his object, and to-day had taken the first step on the road leading to it. He had no wish to judge others harshly, but in this triumphant moment he could not remain indifferent to these various feelings.

Mária Gavrilovna was in the church. Her heart beat faster than usual when the ceremony was being performed over Cyril. It seemed to her in an indirect sort of way that the ceremony was being performed over her too, and when Cyril appeared arrayed in priestly vestments, she thought to herself, " Here I am, a 'mátoushka popadyá' ! " But during these three days she had in some degree reconciled herself to the situation and to Cyril's costume.

After mass Cyril said to her, in a somewhat solemn and significant tone—" Now, Mura, our real life has begun. Up to this time we have only been preparing for it."

For the rest of the day he was in an excellent frame of mind; his eyes sparkled with an inspired brilliancy, as though the ceremony in church had actually transformed him. Mura was frightened at this change, which appeared in a certain degree to further estrange him from her. At times, he seemed to her strange, with the stern look of a priest, and the tone of a preacher. Could this be the same Cyril whom she so loved? At such moments she became melancholy: the future seemed to her uncertain and cold. These passing thoughts kept reappearing and disappearing again from her mind.

The week of probation began. Cyril performed the service every day in the bishop's church. Coming home afterwards, he was usually in a disturbed frame of mind, and expressed his impatience. " How I long to be off to my post!" he kept repeating several times a day; " and how long these preparations seem to last!"

" I cannot understand why you are in such a hurry," said his mother-in-law; "you will soon be bored to death in the country."

" I long to plunge into my work, and to give my whole mind and body and soul to it!" said Cyril, without addressing any one in particular.

Mura's mother shut her eyes, shrugged her shoulders, and went out of the room. "I made a mistake when I consented to his marrying Mura. I can't see any good in him. He talks nonsense. . . . There must be a screw loose in his head," thought she; but she did not tell Mura her opinion.

As soon as the week of probation was over, Cyril began to make preparations for the departure. Mura was ready. He had been urging her all the week to be ready to start at once, and she had packed up her trousseau in a big trunk. On this day, Cyril's father arrived from Ustimiévka. He arranged to hire a conveyance and take their baggage to Lúgovoë; Cyril and Mura were to follow the next day in the post carriage, so that they would find everything ready for them. Early on Monday morning, the deacon having earnestly prayed, started off, and Cyril went to the bishop for the usual blessing.

He found the bishop arrayed in a dark green silk cassock, preparing to go out. Cyril was somewhat surprised at the stern way in which he greeted him. He did not smile or joke, and generally behaved more like a "chief" than before. Cyril attributed this to his being now ordained, and subject to the bishop's direct orders. He had remarked before, that the bishop behaved more freely and simply to laymen; on this occasion he did not invite him to take a seat, as he had done before, and himself stood.

"Are you starting off to your work?" said the bishop, running his fingers over his rosary.

"Yes, I intend to start to-morrow," replied Cyril.

"Which means that you have not thought better of it, and changed your mind?"

"No, my intentions are unchanged."

"Because, if you like, I will give you a good place in the merchants' church."

"Thank you very much, but I prefer the country."

The bishop knitted his brows, and steadily looked him straight in the eyes.

"Are you quite sure of this?" he asked, meaningly.

Cyril was surprised at this, and at the change in his tone.

"Quite sure, your Reverence."

"Remember this, however," said the bishop, with the stern tone of a chief, "that in your newly-acquired dignity of priesthood there must be no 'ideas.' You must be pastor of your flock and nothing more."

"I will do my best, your Reverence, to be a good one."

"I am sure of that; but don't imagine that all other pastors are not good ones too: it will not do to enter upon service with such proud notions."

All this seemed very strange to Cyril, and each of the bishop's words astonished him more and more. Whence was all this? Who had instilled these suspicions into his mind?

"Look here, my son," added the bishop, in a kinder tone, "you are a riddle to me altogether. There are only two solutions: either you are a good and simple soul, or else you are possessed by the demon of unrest."

"Unrest!" exclaimed Cyril. "You

did not think so before, your Reverence."

At this there was a shade of vexation on the bishop's face. It seemed as though he was somewhat ashamed of this lecture he had given to a man who was not guilty of anything. He smiled, lifted his hand, and tapped Cyril on the shoulder.

"No, I know that you are an innocent soul," said he, in a friendly tone; "but, however, be careful. I know that at the academy you have been in the society of learned people. I respect learned people, even worldly men of science; but worldly ideas are not compatible with the priestly dignity. Serve the lesser brother, 'one of these little ones,' that's a good idea, but drive out of your mind all preconceived notions. And be careful that your good intentions are not misunderstood, for those that don't understand frequently put a bad construction on good actions. Be careful: this is my paternal advice to you."

He blessed Cyril with much feeling, and even embraced him, and dismissed him.

Cyril left him in a state of perplexity. He had no doubt that some one had been talking to the bishop about him. This "some one," must be a person acquainted with his life at the academy. Who could it be?

He hired a conveyance and returned to the cathedral house. Just as he was starting from the bishop's, his eyes fell on young Mejof, who ran up to him and said—"They have confirmed my appointment, of course at first only as an assistant, but they will soon appoint me definitely."

Cyril understood that he was talking about the inspectorship. Mejof looked at him and continued—

"And so you are ordained already; you haven't lost much time. I can't make you out a bit."

"How can I help it if you don't understand me?" hastily answered Cyril.

"That is to say, I understand. . . . The country . . . influence on the peasants . . . *et cetera*. . . . Excuse my saying so, but it is very stupid!"

"Good-bye, I am in a hurry," answered Cyril, turning his head, and hastily disappearing through the gate. He did not care about talking to this young man. No matter what subject of conversation was started, it always seemed as though their opinions were diametrically opposed to one another. Their views were fundamentally and hopelessly at discord. And besides this, Mejof was a talkative person who liked to air his opinions with wordy tirades.

"He has been gossiping to his uncle the rector, who has handed on the information to the bishop—that's the history of it," thought Cyril; and this explanation seemed to him to account for everything.

V.

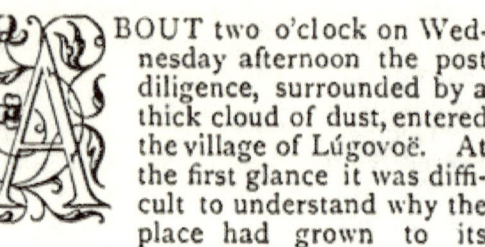BOUT two o'clock on Wednesday afternoon the post diligence, surrounded by a thick cloud of dust, entered the village of Lúgovoë. At the first glance it was difficult to understand why the place had grown to its present dimensions. Perhaps in times past an important trade road had passed through it, which had brought people together at this point; and that since the improvement of communications, the place had been left on one side.

The village of Lúgovoë was about two versts in length and about a verst broad. The huts were stunted, and thatched with old reeds blackened by time. In the chief street stood the church—a small and low building with a single green cupola and without a tower; the bells were hung under a wooden shed supported by a couple of posts. Further down the street, on either side were narrow alleys with huts mostly constructed of mud with low mud roofs overgrown with grass; thus it was plain that the present generation lived in a state of extreme poverty.

At the entrance to the village on the

right-hand side was a garden, spacious but much neglected, overgrown with grass and shrubs, and containing a quantity of high trees. In the midst of the garden stood the manor-house, a square, small, and evidently badly constructed building, with a warped, blackened wooden roof.

The diligence drove up to the church and stopped at a neat little stone house with a green roof, situated in the church enclosure. On the doorstep stood the deacon of Ustimiévka, who was satisfied and pleased with the quarters.

"But the people here are a regular lot of paupers! I much doubt whether the income will be a good one," added the deacon, when Mura had gone into the house to take off her dusty cloak. He told Cyril that he had already been to see the other priest, Father Rodion Manuscriptof, who had been in the place fifteen years, and knew all about the financial aspects of the parish. At first he had received the deacon coldly. "Who are you? Your son, a beginner, is shoved in here as chief, and I have been working away here for fifteen years."

The deacon had explained that Cyril had not asked for the appointment, and that it was merely due to his having come out of the academy so brilliantly. "Oh! he's a 'magistrant,' is he? Of course that puts him on altogether a different footing."

In Father Rodion's eyes the word "magistrant" had a sort of charm, and gave its proprietor a perfect right to the best place. He himself had obtained the rank of priest by means of frequent petitions, for he had not even finished the seminary course. After receiving this explanation, he had become more communicative with Cyril's father and told him that the incomes here were not bad if only the thing was properly worked.

"The people are a beggarly lot, certainly, but there are about ten well-to-do families, and besides that, on Sundays some well-to-do farmers come in, and if you ask them in and give them some tea and *vodka*, they will bring you a regular store of provisions on the following Sunday. We get our living chiefly out of the farmers," added Father Rodion, "but as for Lúgovoë itself 'great is Fedora, but bad.' You can't get much out of it. The people are paupers and uncivilized. There are three "kabaks"[1] here, and they are always full of customers, and the church gets emptier every year. There is also the lady of the manor, a strange sort of person; she never comes to church, and looks with very little favour on the clergy. . . . But take it all round one can live here."

The deacon confided all this to Cyril, and added—"You will get on all right with Father Rodion; and mind you call on the lady of the place—perhaps on account of your position she will look upon you more favourably. Anyhow, she will help you."

After this he hurried off, having drunk some tea, to return to Ustimiévka, saying, that his chief would be vexed with him for his prolonged absence.

---

[1] Public-house.

Cyril, wearied after his journey, resolved to undertake nothing that day. He helped Mura to arrange the furniture and to unpack the luggage. It was a hot August day. They opened the windows looking on to a little plot of ground in front of the house where nasturtiums, dahlias, and pansies grew, planted probably by their predecessor. From the window could be seen the peasants' huts, and narrow threshing-floors where the people were busy, chains glistened in the air, and the sound of them, striking against the floors, was heard. The women raked up the straw and swept the grain into a heap. Mura watched all this with childish curiosity. It was the first time she had ever seen this operation. It did not occur to her that she was mistress here, among unknown people and in a strange place. It seemed to her as though she was only a visitor, and that all this was nothing more than a travelling episode.

Evening came on. They were sitting at the open window in the bedroom, resting after their journey, when they heard the front door creak and some one come in. Mária Gavrilovna looked up at the door.

"Good evening, mátoushka!" said a woman, coming in and making a low bow. She was short, stout, and had a red face as though she had been standing all day in front of a hot fire, her features were coarse and solid. Her bushy black brows met and formed one long line. She had a thick, turn-up nose with wide nostrils, coarse dark lips, a prominent square chin, and a short neck. She wore a handkerchief on her head, which was fastened round her neck, notwithstanding the hot weather.

"And what do you want?" asked Mária Gavrilovna, in perplexity. It seemed strange to her, that any one should walk into another person's house in such an unceremonious manner. She knew that beggars and other suspicious persons do this.

"Welcome to Lúgovoë," said the woman, and again bowed low. Her voice was like a man's. She added, "Can I help you in any way?"

Mura looked at her suspiciously, and did not answer. Cyril came in.

"Well, who are you?" asked he.

The woman bowed to him.

"Good evening, bátoushka.[1] I am a woman of this place, and my name is Feókla. I am a widow. I have always been in the service of the clergy here. I served the deceased Father Parfentii, and also Father Manuil, who was here before you. I will serve you, too, if this is agreeable to you."

"What do you think?" said Cyril, turning round to Mura. "We had better take her on; we have got no one to help us."

Mura called him into the bedroom, and said, in an undertone, "Do you think it's quite safe?—she may have some designs."

Cyril laughed.

"What designs can she have? Look at her. It is evident from her face that she is an honest person."

---

[1] The people in Russia address the clergy "bátoushka" = father.

"Very well, Feókla; serve us well and we shall treat you well."

So Feókla entered upon her new service, and busied herself with the kitchen utensils, washed the floor, and by her zeal, won Mura's gratitude. After this she went away to pass the night in her hut, and Mura gave her fifty copecks[1] which caused Feókla indescribable delight. She seized both Mura's hands and kissed them so impetuously that she quite frightened her. Feókla then thought that she would go and impart the latest information about the new arrivals to her friends. She therefore started off to the sexton's house, as there she would probably find the largest audience.

Soon after her departure, the door again opened, and the creaking of heavy boots was heard. This, it appeared, was the sexton, who was anxious to present himself to the new clergyman, and said that his name was Cyril.

"And you, sir, what is your name?"

"Cyril," answered he.

"Oh, that's easy for me to remember! One does not forget one's own name," philosophically remarked the sexton, adding—"You need have no doubts about your safety; I always sleep at night near the church railings, and in case I wake, I begin to ring the big bell; but if you wish it, I will not do so, as it might disturb the young mátoushka."

Cyril told him to continue to do what had always been done before. Night

---

[1] About a shilling.

came on. Mura, worn out by her journey, fatigue, and new impressions, fell asleep as soon as she was in bed. But Cyril could not sleep. To-day he was as yet a private individual, bound by no actual ties with the new life lying before him; and to-morrow his service commenced. As yet, he was ignorant what this life would bring him. He had no experience to guide him on this point. The examples of clerical life that he had known, had been of a different nature.

So far as he was acquainted with the clergy, the life consisted in one long struggle with the parishioners for income. The parishioners' interest is to give as little as possible, and the clergy, scarcely secure from actual want, to get as much as possible out of them. To earn more, to live better, to provide for the family: these are the inevitable problems.

These thoughts disturbed Cyril. How should he manage to conduct himself? Would he succeed in winning the esteem of his parishioners? Would they think him ridiculous? Tradition is the product of ages. People get accustomed to the bad, just as they do to the good. Tradition has been established by the united efforts of many generations, who have acted at different times, but all unanimously, and in one direction. And he alone was going to draw the sword against this numberless host, against the opinion of ages.

The pale rays of the moon shone into the room through the open window; the distant barking of dogs was heard; the sexton woke up and rang the big bell. Mura woke up for a minute and asked Cyril why he did not go to bed.

"The night is too beautiful, I cannot sleep," answered he; and his thoughts turned to Mura. There she sleeps, with the carelessness of youth, full of life and health. And she loved him sincerely, and her heart was good. And how could he say he was alone, with such a creature with him? Would she help him? Would she encourage him? He could not answer these questions which presented themselves so clearly to him for the first time. God only knew what she expected, and what would happen.

"Go to bed, Cyril!" muttered Mária Gavrilovna, half opening her eyes; and this seemed to Cyril like an answer to his doubts. No, there was nothing to fear from that quarter. She loved him. All her joy was concentrated in him. And she would go with him, hand in hand, whatever happened.

At nine o'clock the following morning the churchwarden informed him that the deacon and the clerk were waiting for him in the church.

"Yes, and the churchwarden has arrived. Only Father Rodion is not there. Perhaps you wish to see them."

Cyril considered it his duty to call on Father Rodion personally. So he dressed himself in his cassock, and ordered the churchwarden to conduct him to the priest's house.

Father Rodion lived in a private house which he had built himself, as he explained, in order that after his death, his wife and numerous daughters should have somewhere to lay their heads.

"And in the church-house, you know, a new man comes, and turns them out into the street."

So he had magnanimously surrendered his half of the church-house to his colleague. His house stood near the stream, separated from the peasants' huts, and distinguished by its slate roof and yellow blinds.

Father Rodion was in an embarrassed state of mind. According to custom, he ought first to call on his chief. But considering Cyril's youth, and that he, Father Rodion, had served the Lord fifteen years in the capacity of priest, and as many more in the lower ranks, his pride would not allow him to do this. But he knew that if the new priest sent for him, he would have to go.

Cyril's arrival helped him out of the difficulty.

"I have come to present myself to you, Father Rodion. I am called Cyril Obnovliénsky."

"I ought by rights to have called on you, Father Cyril, as you are the chief."

"In the country it is not necessary to talk about chiefs," said Cyril, in a simple and sincere tone; "let us consider ourselves simply as colleagues, and nothing more."

"That's certainly as it ought to be."

"As it shall be!" added Cyril. "How am I to act as chief, when I amas yet entirely without experience?"

Father Rodion was reserved, and spoke hesitatingly, weighing every word. Who knows what sort of bird he is? He talks very well, but when it comes to actions, it is impossible to foresee what he will do.

As a precautionary measure, he had put on his old threadbare cassock, although he had a new and a good one. Don't let him imagine that he is going to make money here!

For a quarter of an hour they talked about general subjects. Father Rodion asked if it was true, that Cyril had passed the examination at the academy, at the head of the list? Cyril answered it was so.

"And may I ask what induced you to come to the country?"

"Health," answered Cyril: "my health is bad, and the town is bad for it." " I shall not explain to him, he won't understand," thought Cyril, looking at Father Rodion's puffy face and stupid expression.

"Aha! that's true—the country air soon puts a man right!" said Father Rodion, and thought to himself, "He doesn't look very bad."

After a short conversation, Father Rodion's scepticism in this companionship, of which Cyril had spoken, was softened. " He is a strange fellow, but he seems good-natured, and doesn't carry his head too high."

But he had one question, which he considered would be a touchstone of the new clergyman's qualities. When Cyril got up, to go to the church, he said to him—

"Look here, Father Cyril, I had better explain to you at once about money matters, so that there shall be no misunderstanding."

" Well, what is it, Father Rodion?"

" About business affairs. This is how we have always arranged things: two copecks go to the priests out of the receipts, and the third to the deacon and clerk."

"Well, if that is the custom, I shall not change it."

"That's all right! And about these two copecks for the priests—how will they be divided?"

"Equally between us, of course."

"Oh, then, he really is a decent sort of fellow!" thought Father Rodion; "Father Manuil always used to take the lion's share. He really is a good sort."

From this moment, Father Rodion's expression lit up, and he became more confiding.

"You must excuse me, Father Cyril, for not introducing you now to my family; they are not ready to receive any one at the present moment," said he; and after that they started off to the church.

The Lúgovoë parish church was an old building. Its low arches were blackened by the combined action of incense smoke and damp, the paintings of the various sacred images had become so worn out, that only the oldest parishioners could distinguish the various faces represented on them. Everything in the building required complete restoration—the floor, which had not been repaired for twenty years, the chandelier, with the candlesticks green with verdigris, and even the building itself. The church was very small, and could not hold more than three hundred people.

"And it's getting emptier," said Father Rodion, with a distressed air.

On the right-hand side, near the door,

stood the churchwarden, leaning against a pillar, a short, thick-set peasant, with a short greyish beard and with hair carefully combed and greased with olive oil. He was dressed in an ornamented coloured waistcoat, a cotton shirt, baggy trousers, and he had no coat on.

"Karpo Michaïlovitch Kulik, our churchwarden!" said Father Rodion, introducing him to Cyril. "One of our most honoured parishioners. He's a man of property. He has three hundred sheep, &c."

Kulik bowed and put out the palm of his hand to receive the blessing. Cyril silently blessed him.

"Trr—yetie trr . . ." began Kulik, but could not get to the end of his phrase.

"Which means he has served as churchwarden for three terms of three years each," explained Father Rodion. "He stammers." Kulik pulled away the cloth covering from a box by which he was standing, and displayed to Cyril a systematically arranged pile of wax candles of various sizes, from the very thinnest, two copeck ones, to the half-rouble ones used at weddings. Kulik evidently had not served his three terms of service as churchwarden in vain, or, at any rate, he had learnt how to keep the candle-box in proper order.

Cyril had scarcely got to the middle of the church, when from each side of the choir appeared two figures, very slightly resembling each other, but having a common characteristic. The one appearing on the left-hand side was a short man in a grey cassock, with a mass of curly black hair. The sunken cheeks, sharp nose, the yellow complexion, and the unusually thin growth of hair on his face, all bore witness to the internal complaint from which this man suffered. The man who appeared on the right-hand side, was tall and had an athletic figure. He was dressed in a tight black cloth coat. He walked with a firm gait, and the floor creaked under him. They both walked with their hands hanging down, and the unhealthy face of the one expressed the same humility as the rosy, healthy, hairy face of the other. With the same respectful air they both bowed before the chief, and both put out their hands to receive his blessing.

"The deacon Simeon Strytchok," announced the short man in the cassock, with a feeble alto voice.

"The diatchók [1] Dementii Glushenko," said the other, introducing himself, with a deep bass voice.

Having received the blessing, they stood with their faces towards the gates [2] through which Cyril and Father Rodion had disappeared. They examined the altar. Cyril saw that the building was scarcely in a safe condition, and that the ornaments required restoration and renewing.

---

[1] Diatchók = clerk, man who reads the psalms, &c.

[2] In the Russian, as in all Eastern churches, the altar where the priest officiates is separated from the rest of the church by a wall or screen on which sacred pictures and images are painted. There are double doors in front of the altar which are opened only at certain parts of the service, and only priests are allowed to pass through these doors, and also the Czar.

"We haven't got any money, otherwise we should have done it long ago!" said Father Rodion; but, as a matter of fact, such an idea had never entered his head till that moment. He was of opinion it was all the same to God, where, and with what details, people worshipped Him.

The inspection at length came to an end; Cyril invited them all to his house. Although Mura was still asleep, Feókla had got the samovar ready, and so Cyril entertained the whole of the staff of the parish church at tea.

VI.

O Father Rodion's surprise, the church was crammed with parishioners on Sunday. Among the congregation were a certain number of outlying farmers, but the chief contingent of the worshippers consisted of regular inhabitants of Lúgovoë. But Father Rodion's astonishment reached its furthest limit when he saw, while the deacon was reading the gospel, the lady of the manor, Nadiéshda Alecsiéëvna Kroupiéëv, walk in, and take up her place on the left-hand side behind the choir.

There was nothing very extraordinary in this, as all the week a sort of agitation had been kept up in the place about the new priest, not only by the clerk and the sexton, but especially by Feókla. Every evening she had described the new clergyman to an admiring audience of old women; she had told them also of his wife, how they lived and what they said. She had called Cyril, "the kindest soul," and she had said of Mura, that "it was a job to understand her: she was somewhat shy, and had no idea of housekeeping." From other sources it had become known that Cyril was a tremendously learned man. The churchwarden Kulik had said that there were only twelve such men in the whole empire. It is probable, therefore, that Cyril's reputation for learning, had awakened the curiosity of the lady of the manor. All expected that the new incumbent would preach an introductory sermon, in which he would display to the Lúgovoë parishioners his extraordinary learning. They also expected that the learned chief would organize a specially solemn service. But from the very first step disenchantment began.

"A regular lapwing!" "Disgracefully thin!" said the parishioners, in whose opinion a priest ought to be fat, to have a bushy beard, and a loud and deep voice. The ministry of the new clergyman did not please them.

"He mutters something under his nose, it is impossible to hear anything. Father Rodion, although he knows nothing, serves better. One can at any rate hear every word he says. What is the use of this wonderful learning?"

When mass was ended, and the new incumbent had delivered no sermon, the disenchantment was complete.

"A fine sort of learned fellow! He was evidently so incapable that they sent him to us. There are only twelve such in Russia, they say: I think one could find twelve thousand—there are too many of them."

Father Rodion stood all the time during mass with his face to the altar. He afterwards went up to Cyril and quietly said to him, "Father Cyril, the lady of the manor is in church. This is an unusual event. I think you ought to take the *pain béni* to her."

Cyril knew well from childhood of this custom of taking the bread to the squire, and it was a custom that he did not at all like.

"No, Father Rodion, it is unnecessary," said Cyril; "I know nothing as yet about her worthiness ... and do you know either, Father Rodion?"

"That's nothing to do with it.... But she is the lady of the manor, and I always take her the *pain béni*."

"Excuse me, Father Rodion, but I shall not do so," quietly remarked Cyril.

The more observant parishioners remarked that he did not carry the *pain béni* to the lady of the manor. They also noticed another incident. When the service was ended, the farmers harnessed their horses into their *dilijani*[1] and set off home again. The other various local well-to-do people dispersed. Cyril invited no one to drink tea or take *zakouska*[2] with him. This circumstance gave rise to a considerable difference of opinion. Some said he was proud, and others thought that this showed that he wished to be impartial to all his parishioners. They watched the expression of the lady of the manor's face, to see if the inattention of the new clergyman had offended her, but there was no trace of such an

---

[1] Dilijan, a conveyance used by the farmers in Little Russia.

[2] Zakouska, a sort of impromptu meal, consisting of vodka, cheese, caviare, and other cold things—generally a prelude to a regular meal.

expression. She came out of church, spoke for a moment with two women—as it appeared afterwards, to ask their names—got into her carriage and drove home.

It can easily be imagined that on that day, the conversation centred chiefly on the new priest, and it must be added that criticism was, on the whole, unfavourable.

But on this day a circumstance occurred which completely dumfounded the parishioners of Lúgovoë.

Anton Bondarénko, whose mud hut was situated on the outskirts of the village suddenly wished that his daughter should be married at once. This was somewhat strange, seeing that the season for marriages usually begins at the end of September. But altogether unexpected circumstances had made this a matter of immediate necessity. When this became evident, Marko Pratzuk, a fine young fellow put aside his business for the moment and sent his relations to Anton, to arrange about the marriage. As the new clergyman's turn for taking the services for that week had begun that Sunday, Anton went to Cyril. This was at seven o'clock in the evening. Cyril, who had only just finished the evening service, had returned home and found Mura at the tea-table.

"Is the bátoushka at home?" asked Anton of Feókla, who now considered herself quite established in the parsonage kitchen.

"He's drinking tea. You must wait!"

"It will be dark when I go home; you know it is two versts off."

"I can't disturb him when he is at table.... He's only this minute come in from church."

This conversation took place in the vestibule. Cyril heard every word of it. He opened the door, and turned to Anton.

"What do you want?"

Anton took off his hat and bowed. "I've a favour to ask of you, bátoushka. It's on business."

"Come into the room," said Cyril. Anton entered and bowed to Mária Gavrilovna.

"Well, what is it?"

"My daughter must be married!... So I've come..."

"Very well, we'll marry her, whenever you like!

"Would to-morrow do?"

"Perfectly. To-morrow it shall be! Come to church at ten o'clock."

Anton bowed again, and was silent.

"Well, go, and God be with you!" said Cyril. But Anton did not show the least sign of moving. He did not consider their business ended, he did not even consider it begun. He had not reached what was, in his opinion, the chief point. He had not the least doubt that the bátoushka would be willing to marry his daughter.

"But how much will it cost for the wedding, bátoushka?" asked Anton, at length.

"Oh, you just give one hundred roubles," said Cyril, looking at him in the most serious way straight in the eyes. Anton smiled sarcastically, and expressively shook his head.

"H'm! . . . Such a sum I've never even seen from my birth."

"Very well, I shall not take less."

Anton lifted his eyes, trying to gather from Cyril's expression whether he was joking or naturally stupid. "He must be a joker," thought Anton to himself, and said—

"No, bátoushka, let me hear the real price."

"What's your name?" asked Cyril.

"Anton Bondarénko."

"Well, look here, Anton, you ask for the real price when you go to the market; you wish to buy a pig, they tell you the price; but you've come to me about a church affair, a sacred affair. The church is not a market, and there can be no trading in it."

Anton looked at him with an uneasy glance. "Well, I shall not hurry," thought Anton to himself. "Is he avaricious? the Lord only knows him."

"Well, go, with God!" added Cyril. But Anton did not move.

"How is it to be, bátoushka?" asked Anton.

Cyril returned to the table, sat down and took up a glass full of tea.

"Have you much land?" asked he.

"Land?—four and a half dessyatines" (twelve acres), "and besides that half a dessyatine where reeds grow."

"And what sort of crop have you had?"

"Well, what shall I say? It was neither one thing nor the other. From two dessyatines of rye I got about ninety-two bushels.[1] Half a dessyatine

---

[1] This is about seventeen bushels an acre.

of barley gave me **twenty-eight** bushels.[1] Half a dessyatine of water melons—nothing very special, they hardly repaid the labour spent upon them. And the dessyatine of wheat which I sowed never even appeared above the ground. But the hay in our parts nearly always turns out well. Tall and thick. . . . God grant that there may be such hay in all the world! I assure you, bátoushka, it is not hay; what should one call it?—silk."

"So you are quite a rich man, Anton. Why should I not take one hundred roubles from you?"

Anton opened his eyes wide. He could not detect the fine tone of banter with which Cyril said these words. Seeing his doubts, Cyril said straight out—"Well, now go, Anton. Give me what you can for the wedding. And even if you can't give anything, I will do it all the same. And tell all your friends not to bargain with me."

Anton thanked him and went out in a very disturbed frame of mind. He could not make up his mind whether to speak to the others about his conversation with the new priest, or not. But as he went along, he reckoned that he could, without hurting himself, give a silver rouble for the wedding, exclusive of candles, which he would buy separately. He could not have done it for less than five roubles with Father Rodion, and with candles it would have run to seven. This thought was so pleasant to him that he became afraid that something might stop it, or that

---

[1] Nearly twenty-one bushels per acre.

the clergyman might change his mind. Evidently the new man was simply ignorant of the ordinary methods of procedure in such cases. And if the affair reached Father Rodion's ears, the latter would probably explain to the new priest, and the affair would then end less favourably for him, Anton. He therefore decided to keep the thing secret, at any rate, till after the wedding. And when he was asked what the new bátoushka had taken for the wedding, he said, without the least hesitation, " He screwed out six silver roubles."

"Aha! evidently he knows his affair."

"And why not?" said Anton, finally stifling his conscience. " You must pay for his reputation of being learned, very learned."

As soon as Anton had gone out and shut the door behind him, Cyril got up and paced about the room in an agitated manner.

" It is simply disgusting how deeply rooted this malady is in their souls!" said he, turning to Mura. " He comes straight to me as he would to a shopkeeper: your merchandize, my money! And I am certain that he is discontented and even agitated. . . . No, look here: I am a clergyman, I have to solemnize the bond between his daughter and her *fiancé;* he comes to me about this; he says to me, ' Sell me God's blessing for five roubles!' I ought to say to him, ' No, I can't, it costs ten,' and at length, after a lot of bargaining, we should agree for seven roubles, fifty copecks. . . . What sort of opinion must he have of me?"

"But still, Cyril, the clergyman has

got to live somehow," replied Mária Gavrilovna.

"Certainly, Mura, certainly! But it must be arranged somehow differently. Such an arrangement is insulting to me—insulting!"

Mura replied nothing to this, but still Cyril had not in the least degree succeeded in convincing her. From her earliest years she had seen how the clergy quietly bargain over the various demands made on them, and had accustomed herself to look on this as in the natural order of things, and that it could not be otherwise.

The next day the marriage of Garpina with Marko Pratzuk took place. There were very few people there, partly on account of the heat of the weather, and partly because the real truth about Garpina was generally known. The young people were in a hurry, as they wished to get to work on the threshing-floor, and intended to assemble again in the evening for a feast. After the wedding Anton went up to Cyril, and, with a very confused look, said—"As you settled it, bátoushka, here ... I can pay one rouble."

Cyril quietly took the rouble note from him, and at once gave it to the deacon, Father Simeon. The latter looked at the note, and, quite unconsciously, made such an ugly face that the diatchók Dementii who was at that moment carrying the crowns[1] to the altar, immediately understood that something had happened which was not usual.

---

[1] In the Orthodox Church crowns are worn by the bride and bridegroom during a wedding.

Half a minute later they were whispering together about something in the choir; the sequence of which was that Dementii crossed the church with rapid steps, caught up Anton at the door as he was going out and seized him by the arm.

"You ox-headed fellow, have you lost your wits?" asked he, in a low, contained tone.

"What about?" asked Anton, who knew what he meant perfectly well.

"Come! don't pretend you don't know what it is about: you've paid a rouble for the wedding, have you?"

"I swear to you, Dementii Ermilitch, it's all I've got."

"I don't ask you how much you've got, but I want to know what sum the new bátoushka asked."

"The bátoushka? . . . the bátoushka said, 'Give what you can,' . . . and so . . . I . . ."

The diatchók was completely taken aback by this. Anton in the meanwhile slipped off. Dementii returned to the choir with more sedate steps, and told the deacon about his interview with Anton. At this moment Cyril, who had taken off his vestments, came out from the altar, and directed his steps towards the entrance. They were silent, but on their faces was plainly written discontent and surprise, although they tried to conceal these feelings. Cyril remarked this, but, looking as if he did not, went out of the church.

"Now, what does this mean, Father Simeon, I only ask you?" cried the diatchók Dementii with all his powerful voice. "We shall die of hunger! If we don't get money for weddings, where are we to get it?"

"This is the new order of things, Dementii Ermilitch," answered the deacon, in a weak little tenor voice, and added—"Take away the ladle with the wine, Dementii Ermilitch."

The diatchók darted towards a little square table standing in the centre of the church, caught hold of the ladle, and started off to the altar with it, not disguising his feelings of disgust.

The deacon stood quietly with his head bent down, like a man who is accustomed to humble himself before all the possible misfortunes of life.

"I tell you what it is," said the diatchók, turning round from the altar; "let's go to Father Rodion, and tell him."

"Yes, we really must," answered the deacon, and they both went out and started off to Father Rodion.

VII.

ATHER RODION received them without ceremony. He was dressed in wide nankeen breeches, low boots, and a short jacket. When they entered the room which he called his parlour, Father Rodion was standing by a cage near the window and carefully changing his canary bird's water.

"Ah! welcome our forces!" said he, continuing his occupation. "Well, how are affairs?"

"Bad, Father Rodion!" complained the diatchók Dementii, in whose breast there was still great vexation.

"Well, what is it?"

"We have this minute married Anton Bondarénko's daughter, and we got a rouble for the wedding!"

"How did that happen?"

Father Rodion still kept calm, and continued his idyllic operation.

"Very simply. We finished the wedding. Anton comes up to Father Cyril . . ."

The diatchók began to relate how the affair stood, and told every detail. When he arrived at Anton's explanation and repeated his answer: "'The bátoushka,' says he, 'said, Give what you can,' says he," Father Rodion suddenly left the cage, which began to swing from side to side.

"Ah, that's it, is it? Well, that *is* bad," said he.

"Very bad," mournfully repeated the deacon.

"It is only necessary for such a thing to happen once, and every one knows about it. This will please 'them' very much."

By "them," Father Rodion meant the parishioners. He asked his visitors to sit down, and a council of war was held.

"I confess I noticed something . . . something . . . suspicious about him from the very first," said Father Rodion. "If he continues in this way we shall have to complain to him about it."

The council lasted an hour, and it was eventually decided to do nothing in a hurry, but to watch the progress of events and see what turned up. It might be nothing but want of experience—simply a man who did not know business matters.

Many and various applications were made to Cyril during his first week for taking the services. Pachom, the blacksmith, who shod the whole country around, lost his mother, a very old woman. The blacksmith was not especially distressed about this, as she had been ill for a long time, and had given him no help, and had merely been another mouth to feed in addition to the seven of his own family. He went straight to the diatchók Dementii.

"What, has Mavra given up her soul to God?" asked Dementii.

It was well known in the village that Mavra was in a bad way. The blacksmith, moreover, would not have wasted his time with the diatchók at such a busy season, without good reason.

"It is as you have guessed, Dementii Ermilitch. She has indeed given up her soul. May hers be the kingdom of heaven!"

"Well?"

"We must bury her."

"Very well, go and bury her, and we will come to the cemetery on Sunday and sing. Maybe by that time the Lord will have taken some one else; so that we can do them together."

"I want the thing to be done properly, Dementii Ermilitch."

"Yes, I should like to be a bishop, goodness only knows! Your Mavra was not a big bird! You would like, forsooth, to have her buried by the whole staff from the cathedral for four greevens!"[1]

"But, Dementii Ermilitch, I will pay my utmost. Perhaps some day I may have to shoe a horse for you."

"Oh no, you won't get round me that way, Pachom! I haven't even threshed my corn yet."

"In that case I must go to the bátoushka himself!" and Pachom started off to Cyril.

"They have already got wind of what sort of fellow the new bátoushka is. They won't go to Father Rodion on any

---

[1] About a shilling.

account," thought Dementii, and determined to await Cyril's decision.

Pachom explained to Cyril that his mother had died yesterday, and said he had come to make a petition for the funeral.

"Have you got everything ready?" said Cyril.

"Everything as usual."

"Very well, call the deacon and the diatchók . . ."

Pachom broke in, "The diatchok says, 'You dig,' says he, 'the hole, and we will come and sing on Sunday. I've got my threshing to do,' says he, 'and can't throw it up for four greevens.'"

Cyril said nothing, but put on his cassock and his hat and went out. From the door could be seen Dementii's threshing-floor. The diatchók was dressed in a cotton shirt without a coat. On the back of his head he wore a straw hat. He was busily engaged in threshing with a chain, and the sweat was running down his face. Seeing Cyril come out of his house, he redoubled his exertions.

Cyril stopped for a minute, and thought, "Really, he has a big family."

He passed his garden, entered the wicket gate, and approached Dementii's threshing-floor. The diatchók stopped and respectfully took off his hat.

"God be with you," said Cyril.

"Do you wish me to go to the funeral?" asked Dementii.

"No, it's not necessary; I will perform the service alone. I think the deacon is also occupied."

"He is getting water melons."

"Very well, I will do it myself," said Cyril.

At this moment the sexton brought him a bundle containing vestments. Cyril took the bundle and started off after Pachom.

Dementii looked at him as he went, and thought, "Well, you are a queer fellow! Either God is in your heart, or you are a humbug! I can't make you out!"

Cyril performed the funeral service over Mavra, and at the end of the ceremony when the blacksmith offered him a pile of coppers, he refused to take them. He had only a few minutes previously seen the wretched circumstances under which Pachom and his numerous family lived.

"How can I take money from a beggar?" thought Cyril to himself; and said—"In the winter I shall have a conveyance, and when the tire comes off the wheel, I shall bring it to you to put right! . . ."

"I would do anything for you, bátoushka, in return for your goodness," said Pachom, with great emotion. He was indeed very much touched by the new clergyman's kindness. Things had been hitherto so arranged in Lúgovoë that a special funeral service for one person had always been looked upon as a sign of wealth. Cyril's predecessor had said straight out—"For less than two roubles I don't move." It was considered sufficient in the case of paupers that they should be carried to the cemetery and interred by their relations, and in course of time, when half a dozen had been buried in this fashion, that the one service should be read over them all together. This used especially to be done during the summer-time, when the clergy were all busy with their agricultural operations. The parishioners had grown accustomed to this plan, which had been practised from time immemorial, and they did not protest. There were, indeed, solitary instances of attempts being made to induce the clergy to make exceptions in the cases where a respected member of a poor family had died, as had happened with the blacksmith Pachom. Occasionally, in a happy moment, they had induced the clergy to come out for a rouble by the promise to bring them a measure of wheat when the threshing was over. But generally speaking, the question of payment had hitherto been put in a very plain and unmistakable way.

This happened on a Friday. On the same day a well-built *dilijan*, harnessed with a pair of good horses, pulled up at the door of Dementii's hut. On the front part of it sat a boy wearing a white cotton shirt and a straw hat. In the back part of the carriage, which was hung on springs, was seated a heavily-built peasant with a strong, dark face, with small eyes and thick grey brows. This man was dressed in a blue overcoat, a red sash, and a cap of blue cloth, and he had altogether the air of a townsman. When he got down from the carriage it was seen that he was not tall, and walked heavily and confidently. Dementii, who at that moment was brushing up the grain into a pile on his threshing-floor, when he saw him immediately went to meet him.

"Marko Andréëvitch, why has God sent you? Is all well down at your farm? Come in. . . ."

Dementii both spoke and looked wonderfully polite. Evidently Marko Andréëvitch Shibenko, the rich farmer parishioner, was a very welcome visitor. The farmer's moustache slightly moved, which meant a smile, and he stretched out his tawny hand to Dementii.

"We live, Dementii Ermilitch, thanks to your prayers!" ejaculated Marko, abruptly, and stammering slightly. "Ah! may I come in? . . . Mitka, bring one of the sacks into the vestibule."

"Oh, that's very kind of you; you don't forget us."

Mitka began to descend lazily from his high position, and the host and guest went into the hut. In the vestibule they met Dementii's wife. Antonina Egorovna was still a fairly young woman, and had as good a complexion and healthy a look as her husband. She was busy making up a fire under some pots in which living crabs were moving. She was surrounded by dirty children with naked feet, dressed in long sacks without belts. Antonina excused herself from shaking hands on the ground that they were covered with soot.

"You will not be offended," added Dementii; "she always goes about anyhow here."

A few minutes later, Antonina had washed her hands, tidied the room, and had put the decanter with *vodka* and some fish on the table.

"Whose week is it now for taking the services?" asked Marko Andréëvitch first of all.

"The new one—Father Cyril," said Dementii, waving his arm in a somewhat deprecatory manner.

"Aha! so we shall have a chance of seeing what sort he is. I have constructed a new barn, and I am going to put the grain in to-morrow; and as you know yourself, it is impossible to do this without having it blessed, I want him to come and sprinkle it with holy water to-day."

"With great pleasure, Marko Andréëvitch; you, at any rate, do not use us badly."

"I have prepared everything beforehand. Allow me, Dementii Ermilitch; you will hand it over to the bátoushka." Marko brought out of his bosom a purse, counted out three notes of three roubles each, and handed them to Dementii, who took them.

"If only all our parishioners were as open-handed, we should soon grow rich," said he, squeezing the notes in his hand. "It's only thanks to you good people, that we keep alive."

But at this moment a thought came into his mind which darkened his face. "If there is anything good, the new priest is sure to spoil it," thought he; "he will take it and give him change."

"But why don't you wait till Sunday, Marko Andréëvitch? eh?" asked he, not without *arrière-pensée*. "On Sunday, Father Rodion's week begins. It would be a surer thing, I think."

"I look at it this way: the grain is ready; to-morrow we put it into the barn. It's impossible to wait...."

"Yes, yes.... You Antonina, entertain Marko Andréëvitch, and I will go and tell the bátoushka."

"We might go together, and I could then make his acquaintance. I have brought him two measures of grain as an introduction."

"No, you wait a bit; I will go first, . . and then you. . . ."

"He'll probably receive you and your corn in an unbefitting manner, this queer fellow of a parson," thought Dementii to himself.

Dementii went to Cyril, and found the latter at his writing-table. Mária Gavrilovna was sitting on the sofa reading a book."

"Oh, sit down, please; I will attend to you in a moment," said Cyril, continuing to write. "Mura, this is our diatchók, Dementii Ermilitch."

Mura stretched out her hand. Dementii took it in his huge fist, squeezed it, and, from nervousness, shook it with unnecessary enthusiasm. But he could not summon up courage to sit down, and remained standing two steps from the sofa. Mura asked him if he had a large family. He answered that thank God, it was not a small one, and added that his eldest son had already got into the clergy school."

"Well, what is it?" asked Cyril, turning himself round, together with his chair.

"Marko Shibenko has come from his farm, and wants you to go to him and bless his new barn."

"Very well; let us go."

"He is a rich man, the richest of the farmers. He has himself offered ten roubles . . . without my asking. Do you wish me to take them?" explained Dementii, with the air of a guilty man.

"He offered it himself, did he?" asked Cyril, watching his physiognomy.

"I swear to you, Father Cyril, I never even made a hint to him."

"If he is rich, and offered the money himself, why not take it?"

"Certainly; why not? Here it is."

"Put it into the common box . . . and get ready to start."

"Yes, I see through him." thought Dementii, returning home. "'If he is a rich man, and proposed to pay himself'! . . . And isn't it all the same to me whether he is a rich man or not? Are there so many of these rich people about? He offered to pay himself, he said. Well, and this Marko Andréëvitch is a farmer; and farmers are quite another race. If we were to wait for our Lúgovoë parishioners to open their pockets of their own accord, we should have to wait a very long time."

Passing through his vestibule, he saw the well-filled, and carefully-tied-up sack of corn.

"There, you recognize the farmer at once! He brings it himself, no one bothers him for it. And what a fine sack! It must weigh six pouds at least" (fifteen stone). "This means, at the rate of sixty copecks a poud, three roubles sixty copecks in money."

Marko Andréëvitch had already managed to drink five glasses of *vodka*, and only refused another, because he was going to the priest.

"It wouldn't do, you know, to go there smelling of *vodka*."

They went to Cyril's house, and found

him already attired. Mária Gavrilovna was hunting about the next room trying to find a clean handkerchief for him. Marko Andréëvitch entered the vestibule, and for the sake of good manners, notwithstanding that it was perfectly dry outside, began wiping his feet on the wooden floor. Noticing that on his left-hand side were large double doors, and on the right, a low single door, he surmised that the right-hand door led to the kitchen, and took the left. He opened the door and entered. He stopped on the threshold, crossed himself three times, and then bowed to the master of the house.

"I am Marko Shibenko—farmer," said he, blinking his eyes.

"Aha! we are just starting off to you. I am quite ready," answered Cyril, thinking that Shibenko had come in order to hurry him up.

"Oh, yes, I know; but I have come about another matter."

"Sit down and tell me."

"Thank you very much. But first please give me your blessing."

Cyril suddenly remembered. He could not manage to accustom himself to giving every comer his blessing. He used to put out his hand to shake hands, forgetting that no visit could be paid him without his giving his blessing. Marko came to him, received the blessing and kissed his hand.

"And now for business," said Marko, with an easier air. "We greatly respect our bátoushkas, and always try to oblige them."

"Sit down. Why do you stand?" said Cyril.

"Thank you very much," said Marko, accepting the invitation and sitting down. "That which God gives us in His goodness, we divide with the clergy. Therefore, bátoushka, on the occasion of our first making each other's acquaintance, allow me to present you with two sacks of corn."

"For me? Why? I have done nothing for you."

"You pray for us. We keep sinning, and you avert the consequences by your prayers. That's why! Besides that, we wish to show our respect for the clerical dignity. So please don't refuse to accept the two sacks."

"But really . . . I have nothing to say against it; only it seems strange. . . . Very well, I accept, and thank you very much."

Cyril was confused. He had never foreseen such proposals. He knew, however, that nothing hurts a peasant's feelings more, than to refuse a gift from him.

"And I thank you for accepting it. The principal thing is to be sincere. If you don't scorn us, we are always ready to help. And will you allow me to see the mátoushka?"

"Why, certainly. Mura! here's some one who wants to make your acquaintance."

Mária Gavrilovna entered the room with the handkerchief in her hand which she had found, and looked at Marko, who was seated on a chair, in doubt. She could not imagine why he wanted to become acquainted with her. When she appeared, he got up and made a sort of awkward movement resembling a bow.

"And so this is the mátoushka? And how young she is! Good Lord!"

He suddenly went up to Mura, seized her hand and kissed it,[1] before Mura could take any precautionary measure against such an outburst of feelings.

"I am a farmer, mátoushka. Come and pay me a visit, and you will be very welcome. You will see how we will receive you! . . . We have a great respect for the clergy. . . . We will collect all the people together, and give you five loads of grain; only come!"

This was all very strange for Mura; she could not understand why he invited her so warmly. Why should she go to his farm? and why should he give her corn? She was silent, and looked at him with an air of ill-concealed amazement.

"Thanks, thanks!" said Cyril, for her, "it's time for us to be off."

Marko repeated his invitation once more, and started off after Cyril. At the door he stopped, and cried out in the direction of Dementii's hut—"Hullo, Mitka! come here and bring the bátoushka the two sacks that are in the cart."

Mitka got down, bridled the horses, and a minute later, the *dilijan* began creaking in all its various parts. Mitka reached the piece of ground in front of the house and entered the wicket-gate. He carried the sacks into the house, and began arranging the hay in the conveyance for the convenience of the passengers. Dementii appeared in a long

---

[1] An almost universal custom in Russia to kiss the hostess's hand.

grey coat, with a bundle under his arm. This bundle contained the vestments. He said that the father deacon was unwell. They took their seats and started off.

The holdings which formed these farms were called after the name of their former proprietor, Choubatof, and this land had afterwards come into the hands of free peasants. The greater part of it was situated at about ten versts from Lúgovoë.

Almost all these farmers owned their land; some had twelve dessyatines,[1] some two, and there were two men, Gubar and Shibenko, who owned as much as thirty each, and hired thirty or forty more on rent from the Lúgovoë lady of the manor. Notwithstanding this, their houses were not very luxurious, and half of them lived in mud huts. The other half had managed to construct peasants' huts, with slate roofs, consisting of two small rooms—one for every day, and the other for state occasions, with an additional room for young fowls, calves, and pigs. When these farmers, who were all rich men, were asked why they did not build themselves good houses, they used to reply—" What's the good of it? We are accustomed to our mud huts. The family is lost in the various corners of a big house. In a small mud hut, they are all in a pile; it's warmer and cosier."

In front of these small huts stood high barns, spacious yards for cattle, and for sheep in the winter, &c. It might almost be imagined, that these latter were the real proprietors, and

---

[1] Dessyatine = 2·7 acres.

that the people lived there merely in the capacity of humble attendants on them, making shift in ill-constructed huts and mud erections.

Immediately after the *dilijan* had ascended the hill and gained the elevated plateau over which the high-road ran, the farmers' huts could be seen here and there amidst the endless fields. One might have counted forty farmyards with kitchen-gardens, surrounded by hay and straw stacks. Each yard had its well, and the long, thin poles with buckets at the end lifted in the air, like silent sentinels watching over and defending the farm buildings scattered over the steppes, from external enemies.

Half an hour later, after passing several mud huts, they arrived at Marko's abode. It was in no way distinguished from the rest, but the yards and outhouses were of more imposing dimensions, and the new barn glittered with a bright yellow colour in the sun. There were about twenty men and women standing about in the yard in their ordinary working clothes. They had evidently come here from their work, and had arranged to make a holiday for the rest of the day. Directly Cyril entered the yard, they each began to come up to him in turn for a blessing.

"The new bátoushka," whispered they, among themselves. "And isn't he young," added the women, and for some reason loudly sighed.

Marko then invited him into the hut. In the shady hut, with its low ceiling and small windows, about ten men were seated at a long table, most of them advanced in years. These were the heads of the families. They got up from the table. Cyril crossed himself in front of the dark image hanging in the corner, and bowed to those present.

"How do you do?" said he, turning to them all.

A sort of undefined hum was heard in answer to this. Soon a woman appeared from behind the stove. She had a good figure, red cheeks, and was dressed in a bright-coloured skirt, and a silk handkerchief on her head.[1]

"Ah! here is my wife!" said Marko.

Marko's wife also received the benediction.

"Well, let us go," said Cyril. Dementii unfastened the bag and gave him the vestments. The moujiks looked at him with great interest and thought to themselves, "What young fellows they make 'popes' nowadays." When Cyril had arrayed himself, they all went out into the yard, and here, under the burning rays of the southern sun, in front of a little table, on which stood a pan filled with water, the consecration of Shibenko's new barn was performed.

"And now let us come and eat what God has given us," said Marko's wife.

Cyril accepted the invitation and went into the hut before the others. Here everything was ready. The table was covered with a white cloth, and on it was spread plates and dishes with

---

[1] Married women among the peasants always have their heads covered.

broiled fish and pies made without meat, as it was fast time. Two heavy, square bottles of *vodka* overshadowed the eatables.

"Please sit there, bátoushka," said the host, pointing to a place under the corner where the sacred images hung, the place of honour. Cyril sat down, and next to him Dementii. Fifteen men and two women sat down to table.

"You must begin with a glass of *vodka*," said Marko and his wife together. The latter had not seated herself at the table, and she poured out a glass for Cyril and afterwards for all the rest. All drank off their glasses at a gulp except Cyril, who sipped a quarter of its contents and then put it down.

"I say, bátoushka, what does this mean? You must drink it off!" said the host, in a decided tone.

"No, it is not necessary," said Cyril; "it is such a fearfully big glass."

"But you will offend me! And my barn won't be full! This is quite certain!"

"What have we just been praying God for? Wasn't it that your barn should be full?" asked Cyril, seriously.

"Certainly."

The moujiks looked up from their plates with serious expressions and were silent, and Marko repeated "Certainly;" but his confusion soon passed away and he said—"And, in the second place, that God will give me grain to fill my barn in the future." Saying this, he began filling the glasses a second time. Dementii stretched out his hand with his glass, but Cyril said—

"In my opinion one glass is enough for a man."

The moujiks looked at each other in blank astonishment. Dementii withdrew his hand from the glass and began to run it through his luxuriant beard. But the host took this speech as a joke, and said—"And now, bátoushka, drink another glass, for otherwise the rest will not drink."

"Why should I drink when it is disagreeable and harmful to me? Besides that, to drink *vodka*, is not suitable for a clergyman."

"Our bátoushkas always drink in first-rate style," interrupted one of the guests. Some looked at the speaker in an encouraging way, but others seemed to feel that he had said a stupid thing and looked confused.

"I don't consider a man a bátoushka at all, who will not drink with us!" ejaculated another guest. This was followed by a profound silence.

"What's your name, and where is your hut?" asked Cyril, turning to the author of the latter sentiment.

"Sidor Tovkatch, and my hut, bátoushka, if you will do me the favour to visit it, is the third from Marko's hut," answered the moujik.

"Well, now I shall know, and keep away from Sidor Tovkatch's hut. I cannot drink *vodka*, which means, according to his opinion, I am not a bátoushka."

Sidor reddened to the ears, and was so overwhelmed that he could find nothing to say. Cyril continued—
"But to those who are willing to consider me as a bátoushka, although

I don't drink *vodka*, I will give my reasons for not drinking. In the first place I value my health, and wish to remain long on the earth, and besides that I wish to be always a sensible man; and if one drinks more *vodka* than is good for one, it injures the health and shortens life. You are ordained to live seventy years, if you drink much *vodka* you will only last fifty. You may be a sensible man, and people may respect you, but *vodka* blunts your mind and fogs it, and instead of being a man of sense you become a fool, and all laugh at you. Judge, therefore—what do I gain by drinking *vodka* ?"

"Certainly there is not the slightest advantage in it," remarked some one.

The confused hosts offered no one any more *vodka*, having made up their minds that the regular festivities must be deferred until after the bátoushka's departure.

After they had eaten tart with cream, Cyril got up, and all the others after him. When he had gone out of the hut a sort of subdued conversation began : "What a wise man—truly learned! What does it matter about his youth ? And so serious ! And one may say that our Tovkatch put his foot into it, from ignorance !" When Cyril was getting into the *dilijan*, Sidor Tovkatch came up to him and respectfully took off his hat.

"I ask your pardon, bátoushka," said he, in a confused voice. "I said that ignorantly, stupidly . . . and I swear to you I do not really think it."

And he asked Cyril for his benediction.

"Come and see me, Sidor; bring your comrades, and we will have a talk. Few among you can read, you have no schools, and you spend much money on *vodka* . . . and you are people in good circumstances!"

Sidor listened to this invitation in respectful silence. Marko himself did not drive Cyril back, but sent one of his labourers.

"They are regular children," said Cyril, turning to Dementii, who was sitting by his side. "Like children they believe everything, both good and bad. Therefore we ought not to lose a single opportunity of telling them what is right, ought we, Dementii Ermilitch?"

"Certainly not," answered Dementii flattered on the one hand that the chief confided this to him, and on the other regretting that he could not stop in Marko's hut. "They are probably praising the new clergyman now, and into the bargain drinking bottle after bottle of *vodka*," thought he, with vexed feelings.

VIII.

"AND now we shall begin to make money again! Father Rodion's week begins to-day," said the diatchók Dementii to the deacon, after evening service on Saturday.

"Yes, Dementii Ermilitch, we must really put on the screw! And we have had such an eventful week, if it had only been Father Rodion's week, we should have had nearly forty roubles in the box. A wedding, three funerals, consecrating a barn, and extreme unction for the old woman Miroshnitchich—all important affairs! ... And we've got in all, fourteen and a half roubles! ... I am ashamed to say it ... I really am!"

In a word, the junior portion of the staff of the parish church were very dissatisfied with the new clergyman's first week. No one as yet knew Father Rodion's opinion on this matter. He received the deacon's report about the contents of the box for the week in silence, and did not even answer Dementii's question, "What do you think of that, Father Rodion?" Evidently, as a man of sense, he had not yet come to any conclusion about the turn affairs had taken.

On the other hand, in the village, varied and animated reports were circulated. Anton having brought the wedding to a happy ending for one rouble, told all his friends the true story. "We sinned in judging him so quickly, and it was your fault, Anton; and after all he is a good sort," said the moujiks.

On Sunday when the farmers came in to church they told one of the Lúgovoë natives what had happened at Marko's, and this gave rise to fresh conversations about the new priest.

But it must be said that the village formed no definite conclusion about his character, they confined themselves chiefly to relating facts about him.

"Says he to Miroshnitchich, 'Old woman, you'll get well, and you'll get up and work and pay me then; but if you die, why then we will settle it in the other world!'" said one of them.

"Oh, he's that sort! ... In the other world ... H'm! ..." remarked the listeners.

"When they buried Proshka, Avdiéhk's boy, she gave Cyril twenty copecks, and when he saw that all the property in Avdiéhk's hut amounted to a pot and a broken poker, he said, 'Thank you very much, but I must give you back some change out of this,' and gave her fifty copecks, and said, 'Go and buy some cod-liver oil for your eldest son, and make him drink it, as he has scrofula badly.'"

"He is a queer fellow! A wise man would not do that."

"That depends. ... Whence come the man's ideas?"

"And he told the farmers not to drink

more than two glasses of *vodka*—more, he said, is bad for you."

"Two glasses is very little for a man—a paltry affair."

"Absurdly little. How, for instance, can a christening go off properly with only two glasses? Or, again, a wedding? ... No, it's nonsense!" ...

It was autumn; the days became gloomy, rain set in. Cyril at the time was busy in the parish. Mária Gavrilovna had only just got up, and was beginning to dress. Feókla came into the room and said—

"A carriage has come, from the town." Mária Gavrilovna's heart beat quickly; she ran to the door.

"Mámotchka!"

And three seconds later she was hugged in the embrace of Anna Nikoláevna Fortificantof.

"What has made you come so far, and alone?"

"In the first place it is not far—some fifty versts; in the second place I have not come alone, but with the coachman."

It appeared that the mother longed to see her daughter, and so had started off to visit Mura, who was inexpressibly delighted at her arrival, and laughed, and jumped, and every now and then embraced her again, and finally cried. "It's from joy, mámotchka!" she explained.

Anna Nikoláevna was contented with the quarters. Feókla rather shocked her by immediately entering into conversation with her and telling her that she was "a poor widow," and had served all the clergy here; when Mura left the room she came nearer to Anna Nikoláevna and said to her, in a mysterious voice, 'Keep a watch on the young people, mátoushka, they don't know how to live; any other bátoushka would have had a couple of cows, and ten sheep, and fowls by this time—and he has got nothing. It's a shame to have to say it: we buy flour! I have never known such a thing before. I have been in the service of three incumbents, and they used to sell flour. No, you must teach them the right way."

Notwithstanding that this information was very humiliating for Anna Nikoláevna, she made a note of Feókla's communication. After living two months in a parish, usually considered a good one, they had actually got nothing!

"But tell me, how do you live?" asked Anna Nikoláevna.

"Oh, all right. I am quite satisfied!" answered Mura.

"But explain a little. How do you pass your time?"

"I read chiefly. Cyril is generally either in church or in the parish, sometimes in the school, and sometimes in the country."

"And you sit here alone?"

"Yes—why?"

"And you have no acquaintances? Isn't there a lady living in the place? I thought he had called on her."

"Who? Cyril? not on any account. He said, 'I shall go if I am wanted; but how am I to know what sort of creature she is?' I have made the acquaintance of the other priest's family—six daughters, absolutely uninteresting people."

"The result is that you are dying of *ennui!*"

"Cyril keeps saying to me, 'Get to know the peasants; you will find them interesting.'"

Anna Nikoláevna smiled and thought, "Yes, he really has got a screw loose in his head."

Cyril arrived, and expressed his pleasure at seeing his mother-in-law. "You see how pleasant it is here in the country. And you will stay with us?" said he.

"No, excuse me; that I cannot promise!" answered Anna Nikoláevna, with a haughty air. The place of living, according to her idea, formed an index to people's social position. The capital in her eyes, meant an exalted position and a good income—the country, abasement and poverty. Therefore Cyril's invitation, in a sort of way, was insulting to her.

In the course of the day Anna Nikoláevna convinced herself, from personal observation, that they bought everything, and that Feókla was right. For every little thing required in the kitchen — meat, onions, potatoes— Feókla had to go to the little shop; and cream for tea cost nearly as much as in town.

"Look here, my dear, buying everything in this way must be very expensive! Have you such a large income as all that?"

"Cyril gives me everything he receives to the last copeck."

"Well, what does he get a month?"

"Twenty or twenty-five roubles." [1]

---

[1] About £3.

"Is that all his income? A fine living indeed! And this after the academy and the examination! And to live costs you?"

"About fifty roubles."

"Where do you get them from?"

Mária Gavrílovna got confused and reddened. "It's all right, mother. Our income will soon increase ... we shall soon make it up again."

Anna Nikoláevna looked at her some time in doubt, and then said, in a sharp tone—"Oh! I understand; you are living on your capital."

"Oh, that's nothing! We shall soon put that right. Only, mother, please don't say anything about it to Cyril; he really doesn't know anything about it."

Anna Nikoláevna answered nothing, but knitted her brows and determined to give her son-in-law a lecture.

The following day, when Cyril went out into the parish, Anna Nikoláevna received several visitors. The first of these was Father Rodion's wife. She was a woman of considerable height, broad-shouldered, and fat. Notwithstanding her fifty odd years, she appeared in a light rose silk mantle with blue ribbons in her hair which did not show the slightest sign of turning grey. It must be said, however, that there was nothing affected about her; the mátoushka merely wished to express her respect for the cathedral dignitary's wife, by this gala costume.

"Excuse me, but I have got to find fault with your son-in-law," began she, almost straight off. "He is introducing new customs; he never asks the parishioners, 'How much will you pay?' The result is, they give a few copecks. Would you believe it?—formerly my husband never received less than 60 roubles a month, and sometimes 80, 100, and even 120—and now 20, 25. How is one to live? I have got half a dozen daughters! . . . This is of course only inexperience. He is a young man—but why doesn't he come and consult Father Rodion and take his advice? Although your son-in-law is the chief, my husband is a man of experience."

Afterwards the deacon's wife and diatchók's wife called. They were so shy in the presence of the dignitary's wife that they could not make up their minds to sit down; they, however, explained that with the miserable incomes they had received since the new priest's arrival, it was impossible to live.

"I understand it perfectly," said Anna Nikoláevna, getting agitated by these various communications; "but you may be assured that all will be put right. I shall speak to him: for my daughter's sake I shall speak."

The women who were, of course, acting in the interests of their meek husbands, went out with hope in their hearts.

"I want to have a talk with you, my dear son-in-law," said Anna Nikoláevna, sternly, to Cyril. It was getting dark. Mura was sitting near the staircase at the tea-table reading a novel. Anna Nikoláevna took advantage of her absence to get this disagreeable conversation over.

"I am at your service, my dear Anna Nikoláevna," said Cyril, good-naturedly. He had a sort of idea of what was going to follow.

"I cannot understand the way you are acting; I don't understand it. You have only been here two months and all are already dissatisfied with you!"

"Not all, Anna Nikoláevna—not all."

"All. Father Rodion is very displeased. The deacon and diatchók both complain that they can't live. What do you mean by 'not all'?"

"But the parishioners? I don't think they have complained to you."

"Do you think I am going to talk with your parishioners? It's all the same to me whether they are satisfied or not! You have demoralized them! They pay what they like now, and the clergy's income is diminished to one-third of its former sum. I can't make it out! It's simple madness!"

"But we get on very well. Thank God, we have enough to eat and drink, and we do not dress in wild beasts' skins."

Anna Nikoláevna looked at him fixedly for a moment, as though to try and make out whether he really was a simpleton or whether he was acting a part.

"Look here, Cyril," said she, lowering her voice, "is it possible that you can live without knowing what goes on under your very nose? Your income is twenty-five roubles a month, and you are living at the rate of fifty. Do you understand?"

Cyril looked at her, reddened, shrunk back, and squeezed the skirt of his cassock, which up to that time he had been fidgeting with between his fingers.

"This is Mura's fault. . . . I did not

know," said he; and, getting up, added—"Thank you very much for the information, Anna Nikoláevna: we will change this."

"I should hope so, indeed!... And I need hardly tell you, Cyril, how painful all this is to me. It is absolutely necessary to make provision for a rainy day. I only advise you."

Cyril looked at the window and was silent. Anna Nikoláevna, satisfied that she had made a strong impression, went out on to the staircase to tea.

"What a long time you've been," said Mura.

"My shoes are so tight, it takes a long time to get them on."

Cyril remained long alone in the room. When at length he came out it was quite dark, and Anna Nikoláevna could not distinguish the expression of his face. The following morning she returned to the town, taking with her the "capital," so as to put it in the bank, where she considered it would be safer. However, she left four hundred roubles in case they were required. Before starting she did not say another word to Cyril, supposing that she had already said enough. But she called Mura on one side and whispered to her—

"I wish you good luck, Mura, and hope that all will go well. But if anything goes wrong, come to me at once. Everything that we have belongs to you!"

"I want nothing. Whatever happens, I shall stick to Cyril," thought Mura; and when her mother had gone, she went up to Cyril, took his hand, and quietly said—

"You know, Cyril, ... I ..." She did not get any further, and turned red. Cyril tenderly kissed her hand and said—

"My poor, dear Mura."

IX.

URA, I should like to know what it costs us to live," said Cyril, one day.

Mura guessed that this was "mamma's doing," but as he had resorted to diplomatic methods she resolved to meet him in a similar way.

"Very well," said she, taking a pencil and paper and beginning to make calculations aloud. Taking advantage of Cyril's ignorance, she put down each item at half its real price, and the result of this calculation showed that they were living at the rate of about twenty-five roubles a month, that is, about the sum they were receiving. There even remained a surplus of a rouble or so.

"Aha! I suppose Anna Nikoláevna said that by way of frightening me," thought Cyril, and he told Mura about his conversation with her mother.

"Well, you see the figures," said Mária Gavrílovna, with a perfectly calm air.

The result of this conversation was, that Feókla continued to manage domestic affairs, and things went on in the priest's house just as before.

Cyril had already been four months at Lúgovoë. His relations with his colleagues had reached the point when Father Rodion, who all the time had been hoping that "the young man will come to his senses," said to Father Simeon and to Dementii—

"No, this is not inexperience, but he is not right in the head! That's what it is."

"That's it, Father Rodion," said they; "and besides that, he is quarrelsome."

"We must put a stop to this!" observed Father Rodion.

"Certainly we must," answered the deacon.

It was, in fact, necessary to do something. The parishioners had not only taken advantage of the new order of things, but they had abused it. Those who were by no means poor, had given a mere trifle for the most important services. Some of them had even given ten copecks for a funeral. At first this had been compensated for, as far as the deacon and diatchók were concerned, because during Father Rodion's weeks they had extorted twice the usual price. But the parishioners had soon found this out, and managed to defer their demands, with the exception of those matters which could not be put off, till Cyril's week. Out of twenty weddings during the whole autumn, only six or seven had fallen to Father Rodion's share, and Cyril had performed the rest. The custom of paying "as much as you can" was very agreeable to the Lúgovoë parishioners.

When Father Rodion had come to the above-mentioned decision about Cyril, he put on his best cassock and calotte and started off to the chief's

house. The first person who saw him was
Feókla. His smart appearance, and the
very fact of his coming, so astonished
her that she ran into the room and
informed Cyril.

"Father Rodion is coming to see you;
he has got on his new cassock."

"Well, I am very glad to see
him."

Father Rodion, walking heavily and
waving the broad sleeves of his cassock,
approached the doorway. Cyril came
out to meet him, and conducted him
into the room. He shook hands with
Mura who was sitting there. Father
Rodion sat down and said—

"I haven't been to see you for a long
time, Father Cyril."

"No, you've only been once altogether,
Father Rodion."

"And you haven't called on me more
than once; when people live in the same
place and often see each other . . ."

It seemed at first as if Father Rodion
had simply come to pay a visit. But
after he had made two or three remarks,
he suddenly coughed very loud and
said—

"I have come to see you on business
Father Cyril."

"Well, what is it, Father Rodion?"

"It's . . . it's an important affair."

Having said this, he took his beard
in his left hand, and turned it upwards.
Mura understood that her presence
was not required, got up and went into
the next room.

"Father Cyril, this cannot go on—it
really cannot!" said Father Rodion, without further prelude. "Judge for yourself:
I have got six grown-up daughters, and

no one seems to want to marry them. . . .
I have got to provide for them, to feed
them, to dress them. . . . And besides
that, I ought to put by a marriage
portion for them. . . . Six! Just think
of it!—six! . . ."

"Well, Father Rodion?"

"Look at Dementii, again. He's got
a heap of children all requiring education. But I say nothing about that. I
merely ask you how he is to keep
them alive."

"Father Rodion . . ."

"No, allow me to have my say,
Father Cyril. You know I am not of a
talkative disposition, and it is hard for
me, but now I have begun, allow me to
finish. I have waited four months in
the hope that you would yourself understand; and now it's time for me to
speak. Don't be angry with me for
this, Father Cyril, but I tell you that
this state of things cannot go on! It
really cannot, Father Cyril!"

"What are you talking about, Father
Rodion? It seems you complain about
something . . ."

"I do. . . . About whom? . . .
About you, Father Cyril! You have
made up your mind that we shall all be
paupers. . . . Up to the time of your
arrival we not only made enough to live
on, but even managed to put a little by
for a rainy day. But now! It's awful!
Not even enough to keep alive. In four
months, Father Cyril, excuse me . . .
you have demoralized the parishioners
and ruined the parish."

"What?"

"Yes, ruined it! Lúgovoë was formerly
considered the best country parish in

the whole district ... and now ... now it is a beggarly living."

Father Rodion had entered the house with a firm determination to be perfectly calm and composed during the interview, but he could not restrain his feelings when the subject of the parish was being discussed. For fifteen years all the clergy in the district had looked with envy on the living of Lúgovoë, and suddenly some youngster, only just ordained, comes, filled with new notions and brings it to such a condition, that it is worth nothing. Father Rodion raised his voice—

"No, Father Cyril, you must give this up! Of course, I know you are young and inexperienced, but as others suffer from your inexperience, I am bound to give you advice."

"Do you blame me for not fixing a tariff for the various demands made upon us, and for allowing each to pay what he can?" asked Cyril, when Father Rodion had at length finished.

"I do—I do!" hastily answered Father Rodion; "therein lies the whole root of the evil."

"I cannot act otherwise, Father Rodion—I cannot. It's contrary to my nature and to my principles ... I cannot."

"Excuse me, Father Cyril. This is not right. You are without children, and we three others have each a family. So far we have lived, thank God, without harming any one. Suddenly you come and say, 'No, this is wrong; you have no right to live, you must be cleared out.' We, Father Cyril, are old residents here, and you are, excuse my saying it, you are a new-comer. We live like others, and you wish to make us live according to your ideas. I ask you, is this fair?"

Cyril did not answer for a minute or two. The thought occurred to him what an immense gulf there was between his and Father Rodion's ideas. Certainly, he had never even attempted to explain his principles to Father Rodion. Let them think this a mere caprice, inexperience, or anything else they like. He knew, that to explain the whole system of his views of priesthood and of the calling of a pastor, would be impossible. This would simply mean to declare open warfare with them.

"It may be unjust, Father Rodion, but otherwise I cannot act," said he, thoughtfully, and with pauses.

"What! you allow the injustice of the thing, and refuse to act otherwise?"

"Yes—yes—yes! . . . I shall continue to act as before, Father Rodion, because I cannot do otherwise."

"But you are not alone. Our fate depends upon you."

Cyril got up, somewhat disturbed, and paced about the room.

"Look here, most honoured Father Rodion, I had foreseen that all this would happen, and therefore I asked the bishop to appoint me to a living in the very depths of the country, somewhere where I should have been alone; but he appointed me to this place. It is not my fault, it is not my doing. But so it is, and so it must be. . . . I tell you straight, Father Rodion, and wish you to understand that I have not come here for the sake of income. I could have had a better income in the town than all your incomes at Lúgovoë put together if I had wished it. Just consider, Father Rodion. A man who has finished the course at the academy, who can have any place he likes in the town, comes to the country. Do you suppose that such a man has not thought well about what he is doing? And do you imagine that after this, yóu will influence me with your arguments?"

"In fact there is no chance for us. Is that so?"

"No, not altogether. Go to the bishop and ask him to transfer me to another place, to some small parish. You may hint to him that I should not be sorry for this."

Father Rodion got up, took his hat and stick, and gloomily said—"Goodbye."

Going out, he thought to himself, "One can only suppose from this that the young man is mad." On arriving home he found the diatchók and deacon Simeon. They were sitting in the vestibule. So great was their mental agitation that they had not succeeded in getting up a conversation, and were both sitting silently gazing at the wall. When Father Rodion came in they got up, and at once guessed that the negotiations had ended unfavourably. If this had not been the case, Father Rodion would have said, "Oh, you are here, are you? I am very glad to see you;" but now he walked past them looking as if his mouth was full of water. Three minutes later he reappeared, having taken off his calotte, and said, "Dementii, my friend, go and harness the bay mare to my trap . . . my man is out. I am going to the lady of the manor."

"Aha!" thought the diatchók and deacon to themselves at the same moment, "affairs have not been satisfactorily arranged." Dementii went out and harnessed the mare, and Father Simeon helped him. Five minutes after, Father Rodion started off in his best get-up, with the *pain béni* in his hand. Dementii drove the britchka[1] in the direction of the park.

Father Simeon returned home. But after an hour or so, he repeated his visit to Father Rodion, as the vehicle had returned.

This was on Tuesday, a day when there were no services. At six o'clock in the evening a horseman rode up to Father Cyril's gate, evidently a messenger; he bowed to Father Cyril, who was sitting at the entrance to his house, and gave him a small, sealed envelope, on which was written—"To the Rev. Father Cyril Obnovliénski." Cyril opened the envelope, and pulled out a visiting card, on which was engraved, "Nadiéshda Alecsiéëvna Kroupiéëv," and under which was written in ink, in a small but firm handwriting—" earnestly begs the Rev. Father Cyril to visit her on very important business. If necessary, a carriage shall be sent for him at once."

"Yes, I have no horses," said Cyril, mechanically.

"Do you wish the carriage to be sent at once, bátoushka?" asked the horseman.

---

[1] A half-covered vehicle.

"Certainly, if it is an important affair."

"Very well."

The rider returned. Cyril could not make out what this "very important affair" could be. It could not be a request to perform some religious function [1]; in that case she would have said so, and he would have to take the diatchók and the vestments.

"What do you think it can mean, Mura?"

"I know what it is. Father Rodion has been complaining about you, and she wants to give you a lecture."

Cyril smiled. "What! a lecture? Is she a diocesan superintendent? I tell you what, Mura—I don't think I shall go...."

"I think you ought to go. Besides that, you have promised, they will send the carriage.... She might think that you were afraid of her. And besides, it's only a request.... It may be something important, after all. And you know... Cyril... I have long wished to tell you..."

"Well, what?"

"You will make her acquaintance, and make me known to her; anyhow, then, there will be some one to whom I can say a few words.... You see I am quite alone here."

The carriage very soon arrived. Cyril smartened himself up, put on his cassock and went out. The manor-house was about two miles from the church, and stood apart from the village. Near

[1] The priests in Russia visit every house two or three times a year, and sprinkle holy water in each of the rooms.

it were buildings and outhouses for labourers, cattle, for grain, and a smith's forge, &c. The house itself could be just distinguished through the trees, with its roof blackened by time. The garden was enormous, but in bad order and overgrown with grass.

The carriage passed the gates, drove through the park, and stopped at the front door of the manor-house. A neatly-attired woman, whom Cyril had never seen in church, stood on the doorstep, and bowed to him and said—" If you please, bátoushka, the lady is expecting you." Cyril gave her his blessing, standing on the steps leading to the door. She then led him into the house. Passing through several spacious rooms, he reached the dining-room and stopped at the doorway. A small round table covered with a table-cloth, with cups and saucers, stood in the middle of the room. On it stood a steaming samovar. A boy about six years old with dark eyes was seated at the table, and near him Nadiéshda Alecsiéëvna Kroupiéëv, whom Cyril had seen in church on the first Sunday of his ministry. She at once put down the cream-jug, got up quickly and went to meet him.

" I am very glad that you have consented to come," said she, with a pleasant, sonorous voice. Her dark complexion had an attractive appearance, and her eyes helped this impression. She was tall and well-built, held herself very upright, and she seemed to Cyril to be of a somewhat impetuous nature. Her general appearance produced a pleasant impression on him. She seemed to be about thirty years of age.

"You told me that you wished to see me on important business."

"Yes. . . . Sit down, please. . . . May I give you some tea? . . . This is my little son."

Cyril bowed and sat down. The little boy put down his cup and gazed with astonishment at the visitor in the flowing cassock and long hair, for Cyril's hair had by this time attained a respectable length.

"This is the clergyman, my dear." "This is the first time he has seen a clergyman so near," explained the lady, and continued—"Yes, this is an important affair. Father Rodion, your assistant, was here a few hours ago."

"And complained about me," said Cyril, smiling.

"And complained about you. He said you had demoralized the parishioners, and that since your arrival the clergy had fallen into a state of destitution."

"And you have summoned me here to give me a befitting lecture."

"God forbid . . . quite the contrary!" answered Madame Kroupiéëv, emphasizing each word.

Cyril looked at her attentively.

"Does that mean that you approve of my conduct?"

"Not altogether. . . . But about that afterwards. I promised Father Rodion to talk to you about this. He was very, very much upset about it. Of course, you know, he won't stop at this, but will go to the bishop. You must bear that in mind."

"I?"

"Yes, certainly."

"I have done nothing illegal, and have nothing to fear."

"Oh! that's your idea, is it? Tell me, is it true that you have passed through the academy and are very learned?"

"I finished the course at the academy it's true, but that I am very learned is certainly not true."

Madame Kroupiéëv placed a glass of tea before him, and pointed to the cream and bread, and said—"If you please, help yourself."

"Thank you, I generally drink tea with my wife."

"Oh, you must make me known to her! May I call on her?"

Cyril bowed, and added—"I am sure she will be very pleased—she is quite alone here."

"Very well; I shall call to-morrow. . . . Well now, what is to be done about the clergy? Do you think that their grievance is a serious one?"

"No, I don't. But of course they earn very little now. Maybe that with such families as they have, it is not enough to live on. But I cannot allow such commercial transactions to go on."

"I tell you what. The evil might be remedied. . . . If, for instance, they had regular salaries appointed to them."

"Where is the money to come from?"

"Well, I might pay it out of my means."

"You pay?"

"Why do you look at me with such an air of astonishment?"

"But why should you pay for a thing in which you take no interest? You astonish me!"

"Ah! the first time you come into my house you offend me." She said this with an air of pretended severity, as though she was speaking to a person she knew very well. Cyril became confused. He had not a very high opinion of his powers of conversing with ladies, and always imagined that a construction might be put on his simplest words which he had not intended to give them.

"Pardon me; perhaps I did not express myself clearly."

"No, no—I was only joking," hastily answered the hostess, remarking his confusion, "I only wished to ask you why you will not recognize my earnest desire to help a good work?—if it's only because I've nothing better to do." She laughed slightly.

Cyril said, seriously—"No, it's not that; I only thought that this was an affair which did not interest you."

They agreed to make an exact estimate of the expense at a future interview, and decided for the present, in principle, that Madame Kroupiéév should appoint a fixed salary to the deacon and diatchók, on the understanding that they took no money from other sources. Nadiéshda Alecsiéëvna also promised to call on Cyril's wife the following day.

Cyril returned home in high spirits. He had come to this place with the intention to work for the good of his neighbours, and it had been a source of great grief to him that the result of this labour, so far, had been to create discontent in the minds of his colleagues. Now the cause of their discontent would

be removed. "I have always believ
that there are plenty of good people
the world," thought he, and when
got home, he sang Madame Kroupiéë
praises to Mura. Mura was very pleas
to hear that she would make the a
quaintance of a civilized person t
next day.

X.

NADIÉSHDA ALECSIÉ-ËVNA KROUPIÉËV had lived five years uninterruptedly at Lúgovoë. Formerly the huge, uncared-for garden, in the midst of which, stood the time-worn walls of the manor-house, had been considered a model garden. In it were thick alleys grown over with lilac; many shady nooks, carefully-kept grass lawns, picturesque summer-houses covered with ivy and wild vine. The garden was famous for its Spanish cherries, which were known in the government town under the name of "Kroupiéëvski cherries" and eagerly bought up. There were also plenty of apples and pears, and they used to grow grapes and raspberries. But all this had been before the emancipation of the serfs, when Madame Kroupiéëv's father was alive and in possession of the place—a man who knew how to get the greatest possible yield out of the land and out of the people. The garden had been his great hobby, and the head gardener was a German. As much care was given to the garden as to "a living man." The garden was divided into several portions, each attended to by a gardener

who answered for the well-being of every
tree, for tidiness, order, and fruitfulness
of the soil in his portion, with his skin
The old squire died five years after the
emancipation. One sorrow after another
had driven him to the grave. The
property passed into the hands of his
son Andréi, who, in accordance with the
new order of things, took part in the
zémskoë sobránie,[1] and was also *juge
de paix* of his district. During his
life the property went from bad to
worse. He was an invalid of a nervous
disposition, an ardent lover of nature
of grass-grown fields, of the shady
garden; but he loved all this as an artist
—a man who could gaze for whole hours
at the landscape, but was utterly in
capable of taking any trouble about
them. The huge property continued to
yield a fair income, but not half of what
could have been made out of it. André
did not trouble about this, and was quite
satisfied so long as he got enough for
his requirements. Half his income he
wasted in an utterly useless manner both
for himself and for others; the other
half went to his sister, Nadiéshda Alec
siéëvna, who lived in Moscow with an
impoverished aunt on her father's side
and supported her and a numerous
family.

Nadiéshda Alecsiéëvna was twenty
two years old when her brother died
Andréi died at the age of thirty-six un
married, so that Nadiéshda Alecsiéëvna

---

[1] A local council, somewhat on the principle
of the French *conseil général*, or our county
council, established at the time of the emanci
pation (1861). The institution of *juge de paix*
was also introduced at this time.

became sole proprietress of the property
This change was not altogether pleasant
for her. Up to this time, she had received ready money from her brother;
and she now had to think about the
management of the property. There
was no one there whom she could trust.
The young girl knew nothing about
business affairs. She did not feel in
any way attracted to Lúgovoë. She had
lived in the large, noisy town since she
was eight years of age, as the old people
after the emancipation had always lived
in Moscow. Here she had received her
education, at first under the strict supervision of her father, and later on with
perfect freedom, because her aunt, who
depended for her income on her niece,
did not dare to interfere and indulged
all her caprices. Her development took
place in a capricious manner, and depended entirely on her nervous and
peculiar nature. During her parents'
life she used to prepare her lessons
carefully, conducted herself quietly and
modestly, rose from class to class, and
was considered one of the best pupils.
After their death however, she got tired
of working, for a whole year never
opened a book, and in the following
year was still in the same class. At the
age of fourteen she seemed to wake up
suddenly, and to her aunt's surprise she
became quite lively and even wild. Her
faculties appeared to sharpen: an almost
unnatural love of knowledge came over
her. She energetically occupied herself with learning, and eagerly read all
books that came into her hands. She
made her aunt subscribe to a circulating library, and devoured book after

book. In her aunt's family, notwithstanding the number of children of all ages, she felt perfectly lonely. This arose from the fact that she was looked on as the source of income for the whole family, and distinguished from the rest in every sort of way: she was given more expensive clothes, a better room, a softer bed, and, moreover, all the family constantly tried to express their love and affection for her. The impressionable child remarked all this, and by degrees came to look upon her existence as something special, or at any rate to consider herself more important than her cousins. In course of time this feeling developed into almost open contempt for her relatives. The greater part of her spare time she spent alone in her room with her books, for which she had developed an immoderate passion. Her aunt's circle of friends did not interest her at all, and she hardly took any notice of them, but she had no opportunity of forming friendships of her own. At seventeen years of age, when she left school, she was quite alone in the world, and her shy nature prevented her from having intercourse with other people. She had a curious sort of knowledge of the world, which comprised almost everything except what was useful in practical life, and a feeling of contempt for those who surrounded her and were nearest to her. After she had left school she found life very dull. Up to that time she had spent the greater portion of her days at school, and now she found time hang heavily on her hands. She made two or three chance acquaintances, and attended courses of lectures, which just then were being organized for the first time. But she got no further with her acquaintances. The opinion of people which she had formed in her aunt's family, she continued, involuntarily, to hold; she looked on every one with distrust and did not get on with anybody. The lectures, too, disappointed her. Accustomed as she was to reading books which can be finished at a sitting, she got impatient with the solid regularity and slowness with which they taught science, and the limitation of each lecture to exactly an hour. System and regularity bored her excessively. She could not bear the stereotyped phrase with which the lecturer began: "In the last lecture we stopped at so-and-so." Why stop? She hated these stoppages. Beginning with the elements of a subject in the first lecture, she would have liked to drain it right off to the very end. At length she got hold of books treating of the subjects lectured about, and got tired of the "course."

At the time that she received news of her brother's death she was in a state of profound discontent with herself and with her surroundings. Her nerves were in a deranged state. She had no one in whom she could confide her thoughts, or with whom she could become intimate. She longed for some change in her manner of living. The news of her brother's death made such a change imperative, as she was forced now to think about the management of the property.

At this time her aunt's eldest son resigned his commission as lieutenant, involuntarily, and suddenly being seized with a desire to devote himself to agricultural pursuits, started off to the south, to Lúgovoë. Her aunt's other children had, by this time, become scattered: some had married and others were at school, so that the house became duller than ever. Little as she had cared about her relations, she had become accustomed to the noise of the children. At this time the idea came into her head that she was perfectly ignorant of the wide world, and that, maybe, this world would be more to her taste than the one which had surrounded her up to this time. Unaccustomed to asking any one's advice, she considered every caprice that came into her head as a thing decided upon. She resolved at once to go abroad; and a fortnight afterwards she was in Germany in the company of her aunt, whom she had almost commanded to come. Her aunt could hardly disobey her, because this would mean leaving not only her niece to the mercy of fate, but her income as well.

For about a couple of years Nadiéshda Alecsiéëvna dragged the old lady about from place to place, staying a fortnight in Berlin, Hamburg, Vienna, then going straight to Madrid, and thence returning to Athens. All this was new and interesting for the young girl, but she nowhere received a sufficiently deep impression to feel attracted specially to any particular place. She still felt a sense of deep discontent with her lonely position in the world. Her aunt was worn out by this rushing from one corner of Europe to another, but feared to remonstrate with her niece, lest she should say to her, " Very well, go back to Moscow, and I will travel alone." She was therefore very glad when they stopped for a whole six months in Rome. Nadiéshda Alecsiéëvna, in a passing fit of enthusiasm, visited all the museums and neighbouring localities of the Eternal City, and studied them with the assistance of guide-books. The interest of studying antiquities completely absorbed her. But this passion lasted only six months, and she again fell into a state of apathy and discontent. So the old aunt had to pack up her traps again. They then went to Paris. Here the wanderings of Nadiéshda Alecsiéëvna ended. Her history in Paris may be told in a few words. Up to the age of twenty-two, she had never thought about love ; the idea that she might belong to some man had never crossed her mind. She had a very cold-blooded disposition. Chance admirers in Moscow and abroad had always been snubbed by her. But this feeling, just like all her other caprices, was aroused suddenly, and when aroused, took complete possession of her nervous and almost wild nature. This was caused by her acquaintance with a certain M. Ténard, who was two years younger than herself, and whose exterior appearance was such as to arouse tender feelings in the mind of a young lady of twenty-four, who had never been in love before. He was tall, elegant, with an open and very handsome face, the swarthy pallor of which, seemed to tell of the mental struggles which he had experienced ; and, moreover, the cheery and frank nature of the young engineer helped on his cause. The old aunt could not understand how it happened, but after three weeks or so Nadiéshda Alecsiéëvna Kroupiéëv became Madame Ténard, and took up her residence in a small house in one of the outlying streets of Paris. M. Ténard, too, did not understand the affair properly. The handsome Russian girl had taken his fancy, and he had, perfectly sincerely, begun to pay his court to her. He soon found out her passion for him, and proposed to her as she was very rich. His parents fully approved of the alliance. They belonged to a middle-class bourgeois family, living on an income of four or five thousand francs a year. Therefore they received the rich Russian heiress into their family with great joy. As soon as they had settled down to live together—that is, Nadiéshda Alecsiéëvna, her husband, and her aunt—they were invaded by various members of the Ténard family. The old aunt was in despair, and remonstrated with her niece, who was inflexible. Nadiéshda Alecsiéëvna seemed not to notice anything. She was entirely engrossed with her new passion, passed all her time with her husband, and never let him out of her sight. They visited all the sights of Paris together, and for her, everything seemed to be concentrated in love for this man. At the theatre, driving, or walking, she saw the whole of the world of Paris reflected in his eyes. She tolerated her new relations, and took very little notice of them. This lasted about a year. She gave birth to a son, and from that time her disposition was entirely altered.

This event seemed to have put an end to the cycle of her love. She became sober, cold, and gloomy, and suddenly showed an inexpressible contempt for the Ténard family, who invaded her house. What business had they there? What was she to them—these foreigners with whom she had nothing in common except her fortune, which they shared so freely with her, to her aunt's inexpressible disgust? Her husband seemed more estranged from her even than the others. Now that her eyes were opened, she only saw in him an ordinary calculating bourgeois of very limited capacities, and she ceased to have the slightest sympathy for him. The result of this discovery was very unfortunate. She asked the Ténards to leave her in peace, took the child, and started off to Russia without saying a word to any one. She went with her aunt straight to Lúgovoë, where she found her cousin, who was managing the property, dying of *delirium tremens*, and sent him off together with his aunt to Moscow, promising to help them, and she settled down in the old house, amidst the neglected garden. She devoted her whole attention to the child's education, made no one's acquaintance, and did not receive visitors. Six months after her return from Paris, Ténard appeared at Lúgovoë. She received him politely, allowed him to live in a separate wing of the house for a week, then supplied him with money, and begged him not to come any more. She then opened business negotiations with a lawyer in Moscow, and at the time of her acquaintance with Cyril, was expecting to obtain a divorce from day to day.

A week after Cyril had made the acquaintance of the lady of the manor, Father Rodion received a message from her, asking him to come and see her. He started off for the manor-house in full hopes that Madame Kroupiéëv had managed to alter Cyril's views. The deacon and diatchók impatiently awaited his return, buoyed up by similar hopes. An hour afterwards he returned home in a very agitated frame of mind.

Dementii did not even dare to ask what had happened, but helped the driver to unharness the horse. The deacon, Father Simeon, made the sign of the cross on his narrow chest and gazed quietly at Dementii and the driver. One of Father Rodion's daughters brought out a chair and placed it in the yard near the door. A few minutes later, Father Rodion appeared, dressed in his indoor costume, which consisted of a jacket and checked trousers. He sat down and looked at the deacon and Dementii, who came up to him.

"Rejoice, O servants of the church militant! You will have great riches!" said Father Rodion, without looking at them, and in such a tone that they guessed there was no particular cause for rejoicing.

"Yes. . . . It's about time!" said the diatchók, in a tone of bitter irony.

"What? Do you doubt it? Look here: the lady of the manor is going to give each of us a regular salary out of her private means. I and the chief are to receive fifty roubles a month each, Father Simeon thirty, and you, Dementii will have twenty-five. Are you contented? ... Eh?"

The deacon and diatchók evidently did not quite take it in, and stood for some time in silent perplexity. What could they say, considering that at the very slackest time of the year they had received twice the respective sums allotted to them, and that during the winter, when there were weddings and *Te Deums*, the diatchók, Dementii, had even earned as much as seventy roubles in a month. This was nothing less than a mockery and an insult to them, and it could not be a serious proposal. To agree to take no money from the people, not to bargain, simply meant to give themselves into the hands of the parishioners, and to fulfil all their demands without questioning. As they did not reply to Father Rodion's question, their answer was clear, so that Father Rodion took it for granted, and said—"I shall go to the bishop to-morrow ... to-morrow! He wants to ruin us ... to turn us adrift in the wide world. ... His little game must be stopped!"

But another difficulty arose here. In order to go to the town, it was necessary not merely to ask leave of the chief, but to explain the object. Father Rodion was in such an evil frame of mind that he did not wish to go to Cyril, or even to meet him. He decided to write to him. So paper and ink were brought out into the yard, and on the spot, in the presence of his subordinates and his wife, who had become red in the face with anger, he wrote—"Most Honoured and Reverend Father Cyril,—On account of urgent domestic affairs I have to go to the government town. I consider it my duty to inform your Reverence of this.—With all respect, I remain, the priest, RODION MANUSCRIPTOF."

The letter was sealed up in an envelope and addressed to Cyril with his full titles and sent to him by the sexton. Cyril read the missive and considered it simply in the light of a notice of Father Rodion's absence: the hidden meaning of these simple words never came into his head. He was heartily glad of the assistance given by Madame Kroupićëv, and to him, personally, fifty roubles a month seemed an ample income; and then he rejoiced at the thought that there would be no more commercial transactions in the parish—and, besides that, that his subordinates would have no further cause for grievance. He had decided to tell Father Rodion about this first, and then on the next Sunday to give notice in church of the new arrangement.

The day following Father Rodion set out at dawn. The morning was cold and a fresh breeze was blowing from the north. Father Rodion was attired in a warm cassock of beaver skin, with his collar turned up, a worsted scarf, a fur hat, goloshes stuffed with some warm material—in fact, in quite a winter get-up. He had two horses, intending to reach town by dinner-time, so as to rest and collect his thoughts, and to go to the bishop the next day. From behind the high turned-up collar were seen his round eyes and thick frowning eyebrows, which were steadily fixed on the driver's back. The whole of that night Father Rodion was in a disturbed frame of mind, for he kept thinking of the speech which he should make to the bishop. "I admit I am not learned," thought he, "but I am old, and they have never had cause to find fault with me. So he must listen to me."

He stopped in the town with his old companion at the seminary, Avxent Lutchkof, the deacon of the merchants' church. They had both been distinguished by their idleness, which eventually procured their expulsion after they had remained for four years in the philosophy class. Father Rodion had, however, managed to become an ordained priest, but Lutchkof lost his wife very early, and in consequence of this, he had to remain a deacon for life. He was a very thin, tall man, with a red face, with very little hair on it. To drown his griefs, he drank a great deal, but had the good sense to confine his excesses to the fortnight in the month when he was off duty.

Father Rodion chanced to arrive during his slack time; and although he tried to explain his grievances to his friend, the latter could not understand anything, and kept repeating every five minutes, stretching out his hand for the *vodka* bottle—"What, Rodia, do you mean to say you are going to the bishop?" and then he added—"Why are you going? I have been a deacon ever so long, and have never been to him.... Why? Because no one notices me now, and once I go there I shall make myself conspicuous, and they will say, 'Ah, you red face! you had better retire.' My opinion is, that it is best never to bring oneself under notice . . ."

But Father Rodion did not
opinion, and the following m
eight o'clock was waiting in th
ante-room with a crowd of othe
He wore his grey, worn-out c
order to call attention to his
His old legs trembled from nei
and his heart beat faster than
the hour approached for the
with the bishop, his thought
more and more cloudy. At
seemed to lose all idea of the
his business, and he thought
not be able to answer a sin
when the bishop asked, "W
what do you want?"

At length the sound of the
slippers was heard in the
room, partitioned off by a da
silk curtain, and the bishop
dressed in a light silk coat, wi
calotte and the rosary in his h
at once began his business v
churchwarden who had com
testimonial. Father Rodion'
third on the list. From the m
the bishop entered, his fears
as always happens at the mo
moments. His previous agit
quite calmed, and instead of tl
had been in his mind, he n
perfectly clear idea of all th
going to say to the bishop.
his turn came. The bishop
him steadily and then said in
tone—"You are not familia
father. It is evident that yo
yourself well, and don't have
to come to me often."

"I would never trouble yo
rence without necessity," sa

firmly; and added, "I am
Ianuscriptof. priest."
e do you live?"
igovoë."
voë . . . Lúgovoë. . . . That's
:o me, but I forget. What
want, Father Rodion Manu-
 You've got a fine, sonorous

ie place where your Reverence
sed to appoint the priest,
isky, from the academy as
t," explained Father Rodion.
vliénsky! . . . Cyril, Cyril?"
I the bishop, and his face lit
i pleasant smile. "Oh, yes;
er. He's a 'magistrant,' very
nd a good Christian too."
servation of the bishop's dis-
 Father Rodion. He had no
Cyril was on such good terms
bishop. On the contrary, he
ned that Cyril had been sent
untry for some shortcoming,
magistrants" always received
es in the town. How was he
is grievance now? And the
if to finally extinguish him,
irning round to the other
'I set up this young priest
nple to all. Although he is a
nt' he chooses a country liv-
own accord, in order to serve
brethren."
itors all assumed a sympa-
, and each one hoped that
i increase the chance of his
 petition being successful.
:r Rodion, who did not take
)ff the bishop, observed that
ddenly assumed a stern look;

and the bishop asked him in a voice—" Does your business concern him ?"

" It does, your Reverence."

" Come along, come along ; rests me !"

And the bishop made a sign Father Rodion to follow him.

Father Rodion was very ple the other room, where there no one to overhear, he would tate to tell him everything passed into the next room, turned to the left and went drawing-room, which was with soft, luxurious furniture gant carved tables, and pictur wall, all of which struck Fathe as being of a worldly natur the bishop stopped, sat down a sign to Father Rodion t seat, and the latter, not darin obey, sat down also, trying, to occupy as little space as po

" Well, father, let me hear it. This young pastor inte very much," said the bishop, fat fingers as usual, fidgeted cally with the rosary.

" I cannot tell your Rever news of a consoling nature ab began Father Rodion, hesitatir he regretted that he had to di the bishop. And then he ga tailed account of all that had h without, however, adding or d anything.

The bishop listened with interest. But his face expresse sympathy nor reproach. Wh ever, Father Rodion, in a wo described the last incident about the salaries, the bishop got up and thoughtfully walked about the room. Father Rodion also stood up. At length the bishop said—

"And tell me, conscientiously, as a priest—tell me, does he instil anything of a dangerous nature into the minds of his parishioners: for example, against the powers that be?"

"No, your Reverence; no," hastily and with warmth answered Father Rodion, "I cannot say that he does. In fact I can answer straight and say no."

The bishop's face lit up again; he went up to Father Rodion and put his hand on his shoulder, and said in a simple, almost friendly tone—

"I understand you, Father Manuscriptof, I understand you, for I am a sinner myself. But you must try and understand him. It is you and I who have departed from the apostolic life, and he, this young pastor, is trying to live nearer to it. Now look at the thing from a spiritual point of view—is he wrong? No, he is right. The lady of the manor has behaved nobly too, and we must send her our thanks. From the worldly point of view, you of course, have a grievance—I admit it, I admit it. Have you a large family?"

"Six daughters, your Reverence."

"Six daughters!" exclaimed the bishop in amazement, and with a shade of horror. "God has blessed you! there's nothing for it!"

And he again walked about the room.

"Yes, yes!" said he, as though to himself, "the antagonism between flesh and spirit has begun! He ought to have gone into the monastery! But then there is his love for activity, his wish to live among people. He would make a splendid missionary. Well, well! and what do you want, exactly? Eh?" asked he, at length, suddenly remembering Father Rodion's presence.

"I place myself in your Reverence's hands," answered Father Rodion.

"Ah! you cunning fellow, what can I do for you? I cannot write to him and tell him to give up his good works, and do evil! Because this is an evil, a real evil, that the clergy traffic in sacred things; but I have to pretend not to notice it, because our means are small, and, besides that, the flesh is weak."

"Your Reverence! He, that is Father Cyril, said, if it suited you, he would be ready to go to another parish."

"No, I cannot do that. It would look like punishing him, and I have no cause for punishing him. I tell you what: I will transfer you."

At this proposal, Father Rodion's face fell, and he answered in a dejected voice—"I do not dare to make any suggestions to your Reverence."

The bishop then looked at his watch and said—"I have been gossipping too much."

Father Rodion went out, having received an order to return home and await his transfer. He wanted to put in a word for Father Simeon and Dementii, but thought it better not to mix himself up in their affairs.

Father Rodion Manuscriptof returned that day to Lúgovoë in low spirits. He had set out for the town in the hope of regaining his former prosperous condition, and now God only knew what would come of the affair. For fifteen years he had flourished peacefully at Lúgovoë, he had started agricultural pursuits, and built himself a private house, now he would have to throw it all up and go to some new and unknown place, and instal himself afresh in his old age. And all this because of a mad "magistrant," who had somehow managed to get into the bishop's good books into the bargain. He did not understand, and did not approve of the favourable view taken by the bishop of Cyril. He had lived many years in the world without hearing of these novelties, without which, all would be well. At home he found his subordinates awaiting him.

"All I have gained is that I am to be transferred to a new and unknown place!" explained he, shortly and sorrowfully to them.

"And what's to happen to us?" asked Dementii.

"You? oh, nothing, I suppose."

The deacon and diatchók went out. As they walked along they came to the conclusion that their interests were the most important of all.

XI.

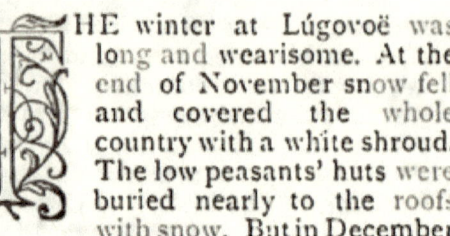HE winter at Lúgovoë was long and wearisome. At the end of November snow fell and covered the whole country with a white shroud. The low peasants' huts were buried nearly to the roofs with snow. But in December it suddenly became warm again; the snow melted, and gave place to a layer of mud on the roads and fields, in which people, animals, and conveyances struggled. Towards Christmas a sharp and dry frost set in, and the regular southern Russian winter began—snowless and windy, not so severe in itself, but appearing so to the southerners accustomed to a long, hot summer. The frost, with short intervals, lasted till February, and then warmer weather set in and the green grass peeped out from the earth.

The church-house was warm. The building was solidly constructed, and the reeds which they used for fuel were cheap; besides which Feókla brought bundle after bundle into the room, and the stove swallowed them up very rapidly. Mária Gavrilovna tried her best to kill time, but was terribly bored. She had made Madame Kroupièëv's acquaintance, but somehow had not got on with her. She seemed to Nadiéshda Alecsiéëvna too simple. After two or three evenings passed together, all they had to say to one another had been said. Nadiéshda Alecsiéëvna from the first, had treated her with formal kindness, which dashed Mura's hopes of becoming intimate with a "living educated being" to the ground. The cathedral dignitary's naïve daughter divided people into two classes, the cultivated and the ignorant, and was persuaded that it was sufficient for two people to belong to the former class, in order to get on well together. But the culture of these two women was so utterly different in nature, that they scarcely understood each other. Mura had finished the course at school, and had read some dozen books which people had told her were good books and ought to be read. All her life she had been under the care of her parents, and marriage had been her first independent step. Nadiéshda Alecsiéëvna had lived an original sort of life, full of various impressions, had learned much, not only out of books, but from life, and, besides this, had formed definite opinions of life and of people. Thus it was that she could only behave to Mura with cold courtesy, and Mura looked on her with a certain amount of astonishment and even shyness.

However, once a week—generally on Saturdays—Nadiéshda Alecsiéëvna and her boy drove up to the church-house. With a smiling face, and without getting out of the carriage, she called Mura to her, who took her place in the carriage, and they returned together to the manor-house. They dined together, and after evening service¹ Cyril came in, and they generally talked till midnight. Mura took but little part in these conversations, and sat silently listening and very much bored.

In January Mária Gavrilovna began to prepare clothes for their expected child. This filled up her days. Her mother sent her a sewing-machine, at which she worked indefatigably.

Cyril was well occupied. In the first place, he was glad that he was alone in the parish. Father Rodion had been transferred to another place a month after his visit to the bishop, who evidently was not in a hurry to appoint any one else to his place. Cyril managed to get through the mass of work he had to do successfully, and fulfilled all the parishioners' demands. Each of these afforded him an opportunity of becoming more closely acquainted with the moujik's existence. He never refused an invitation to stop for dinner after a funeral, or to take something to eat in the peasants' houses, &c. He looked upon these as valuable opportunities for explaining his views on various subjects to them. The peasants got accustomed to this, and listened to him, without that air of formal attentiveness which means that it will all be forgotten at once. He did not preach in church: he considered this kind of converse with the people as fruitless. A sermon is heard

---

¹ The principal evening service in Russia is on Saturday evening, and not on Sunday evening, as with us.

under exceptional conditions. The congregation are apt to look upon the sermon, not as a simple conversation with their pastor, but as a regular part of the mass, which must be listened to in a more or less formal manner. He aimed at having conversations with the people in their homes, amidst their everyday surroundings.

It seemed to Cyril as though his labours were bringing forth fruit. The fact that bargaining for various services from the clergy, had been abolished, was a great consolation to him. The parishioners simply informed him that there was a death, or a birth, or a marriage in their houses, and without any further ado the ceremonies of the church were performed. Cyril also remarked that when the peasants entertained him, the host never offered the company more than two glasses of *vodka*, and that the guests drank the second with a certain air of compunction.

Of course he was well aware that in his absence their libations were on the former scale, and that the public-houses in Lúgovoë did a splendid business. But this moderation in his presence was a promising sign, and he counted on the force of habit helping by degrees to lessen the evil.

Besides his regular work with the church services, Cyril devoted a deal of attention to the school. He visited it nearly every day, and was very indignant with the schoolmaster for not being sufficiently enthusiastic about his business.

"Why did you ever become a schoolmaster if you don't care for the work—

if you have no mission for it?" asked Cyril, when the latter had for the hundredth time expressed his dissatisfaction with his position.

"The mission of each man, bátoushka, is to earn his bread!"

Cyril strongly argued against such a view. He excitedly explained that it was impossible to live thus, that such an opinion might do very well for a shoemaker perhaps, but not for one who made it his business to instruct the ignorant. He even considered it dishonourable to take such a view of so vital a matter.

"Ah, bátoushka!" answered the teacher, "these are the very words I myself used eight years ago, but now I have lived and seen that it is all nonsense. Life alone, is wearisome. There is only one remedy—to marry, take a couple of hundred dessyatines of land, and to farm."

This schoolmaster, Andreï Feódorowitch Kalujnev, was about thirty years old. He came of a middle-class town family, and his father had occupied some small official position; he had been educated at the gymnasium,[1] but had failed to pass the examination from the sixth to the seventh class, and had thrown it up. Three years he kept preparing himself, first for military service, then for the university, and finally entered a factory as a workman. At length he became a country schoolmaster, as that appeared to him the simplest and easiest occupation. About country life he had no knowledge, but he

---

[1] School.

assumed his new duties not without certain ideal opinions. He had heard a certain amount about the peasants, about disinterested service, about the enlightenment of the masses, and these ideas came into his head when he was still very young. But the actuality appeared to him wearisome. His ideas were like straw blown about by the wind, and Kalujnev in course of time became a mere worker for bread and butter, not understanding his business, bored with his occupation, and longing for a change.

Cyril often visited Madame Kroupiéëv. She always received him graciously, and even with pleasure. All her life she had sought after original people, and this country priest was so cultivated that she could carry on theoretical arguments with him. A clergyman waging war against those very vices which had always made her turn with repugnance from the clergy, a man trying to incorporate into real life, ideas which had always been sympathetic to her, was for her a regular find. At first she merely looked on him with curiosity as an interesting specimen of humanity, and was always expecting that he would ask her for keep for the winter for his cows, or hay from a dessyatine of grass land, or else for some other favour which Father Rodion and his colleagues used to beg for. But Cyril asked for nothing. She once inquired if he did not want anything in the way of help in his farming affairs.

"I don't carry on any farming operations," answered Cyril; "and if I wanted anything, I certainly should not ask you for it. . . ."

"Oh, really! Why?"

"Why, you see, thank God, the relations between us are excellent, but directly I take any material assistance from you, I become dependent on you, and you would respect me less."

Nadiéshda Alecsiéëvna was quite delighted with this original priest. On those evenings which they passed together, when Mura was merely a listener to their conversations, she drew him out and made him explain all his opinions about life, and by degrees acquainted him with her whole history.

"I tell you what," said Cyril, openly, after hearing all her adventures in Moscow and abroad; "you have not lived yet—you have only played at living."

He then explained his theory. Life is only possible in the country, where nature is real, where people are real, and where wants are real. To live without being of use to others is thoughtless and stupid. Each man has some little corner in his nature which he can turn to the profit of others. It is unnecessary to strive after some grand work; do something useful, and then, in the sum of human affairs, your existence will stand on the plus side.

"Tell me, Father Cyril, how it is that I sometimes think that you are the first really sincere man I have met with in my life?" asked Nadiéshda Alecsiéëvna once.

"Pardon me, please. There are sincere people in the world; I have myself met not a few!" eagerly answered

Cyril. "You simply have not noticed them because you look down upon them. Maybe I am the first man you have done the honour to look at in the proper manner."

Spring began. In April Mura ceased to visit Madame Kroupiéëv. They wrote to the town for her mother; she arrived, bringing with her a nurse. As soon as she crossed the threshold, her face became darker than night. Her experienced eyes at once detected that the material position of the young couple had in no way improved. Signs of poverty were evident everywhere. Accustomed as she was to notice trifles, she at once remarked a large hole in the knitted tablecloth, covering the table. Nothing was changed in their furniture, but nothing had been added. There were only objects of absolute necessity—tables, a sofa, beds, a chest of drawers, a few chairs, a looking-glass on the chest of drawers, a clock, and an eikon in the corner, and the general appearance of the room reminded one of a provincial inn. Anna Nikoláevna went into the yard, looked at the store-room, at the two outhouses—they were all empty. A few bundles of reeds lay in the kitchen-garden, which had remained over from their winter supply of fuel; there was no sign of a conveyance in the sheds, not even an ill-constructed britchka; and in the other shed, intended for a stable, there were no horses. The lumber-room was also empty. She looked into the cellar, and there was no sign of any bottles—not even empty ones. "They have got nothing, and have earned nothing," thought Mura's mother; "my daughter is a beggar." But this time she herself resorted to Feókla for information about their mode of living. It was impossible, too, to argue with Mura, on account of her position. Feókla's report gave her the final blow: "Good Lord! good Lord!" said she, with the sincerest compassion, "you've no idea of the state of things with us now—no words can describe it! We have to buy everything: we buy milk by the glass, butter, cream, everything comes from the shop!... We have no means to buy cows with! The lady of the manor offered to give a couple of cows—this I know from her head man—but they would not take them. 'I can't accept presents,' said he. If he goes anywhere, he has to take post horses.... Would you believe it, the poor mátoushka grudges every egg she eats?... No income! In the other clergyman's time the walls of the barns were nearly broken down by the grain in them. There was nowhere to stow it all, to say nothing of fowls, and pigs, and calves. But now they get no money. ... That's what we've come to!... The deacon and the diatchók are simply dying of hunger. I am only telling you the truth."

"Oh dear! oh dear!" thought Anna Nikoláevna, in despair; "this is what my daughter has come to!" She thought of talking to Cyril, but decided it would be useless. "I shall simply go to the bishop, and get Father Gávriil to go with me. Perhaps he may be able to bring him to his senses. No, I shall take Mura home with me.... What does it mean? If he wanted to be a saint, why did he not go to the monastery? Why did he marry? My poor Mura!"

Anna Nikoláevna scarcely spoke to Cyril, and tried to take no notice of him, and looked at Mura with an air of grief and pity. Mura gave birth to a son, and her mother stayed for nine days with them. As soon as Mura had recovered, her mother went away. She would not even stay for the christening, but made Mura promise to call the child Gávriil, after his grandfather. She went away, firmly resolved to take decisive action.

Mura and her son both got on very well. Madame Kroupiéëv and Dementii, the diatchók, were the godparents, and at the christening Dementii, who had to stand next to the lady of the manor, became very much confused; but after the ceremony was over, he determined to profit by the occasion, and asked Madame Kroupiéëv, as she was leaving the church, for an acre of kitchen-garden. Nadiéshda Alecsiéëvna at once agreed to grant this, and Dementii was greatly pleased.

Soon after this an event, long expected in Lúgovoë, occurred. One day, on a Saturday, before evening service, the sexton saw a cart approaching the church; it was one of those old-fashioned vehicles on high wheels covered with tarpaulin, something in the style of so-called "fours" in which the Jews drive, sometimes as many as twenty of them in one cart. This *kibitka* was drawn by a pair of horses, and jolted terribly, as it was built without springs. The tarpaulin was turned up on one side, and from behind it, was seen a woman's face with an agreeable expression, with a hat, from under which peeped out hair of a light flaxen colour.

"Where is Father Rodion Manuscriptof's house?" asked the young woman.

"Father Rodion's house?" asked the sexton in his turn. "Why do you want to know? His house is empty, and he has been gone these six months."

The woman's head disappeared, and in its place was seen a man's head covered with a soft felt hat. His face was swarthy and sunburnt. The sexton remarked that his beard and moustache and hair were of recent growth.

"Good day, my friend!" said he, in a pleasant voice. "You are the sexton, I suppose?"

"I am. I'm the sexton."

"And I am the clergyman in Father Rodion's place. Show me where his house is. We are going to live there —I have bought it from him."

The sexton hastily took off his hat, and said, "Very well!" He conducted them to the house, and noticed on the high-road, three carts with furniture and various farming implements. After this he set out for Father Cyril's house, to inform him of the new arrival.

"Oh, he's arrived has he?—that's a good job," said Cyril; and thought to himself, "It will not be so bad this time. *My* system has taken root now."

"They are as young as you, bátoushka," added the sexton.

Cyril replied nothing, but thought

that this was all for the best, as a young man would understand him better than an old man.

The next day, at the time for the Sunday service, the astonished parishioners made way for the new priest as he walked up the church to the altar. He was short but of strong build; on his face was written health and self-satisfaction. His dark lilac-coloured cassock suited him very well. He walked with a slow, pious gait.

Ascending the steps in front of the screen, he made a deep bow and kissed the eikon on the eikonostasis.[1] He looked as if he was going to turn round to the congregation and preach a short sermon, or at least say, " I am the priest, Makárii Siloámski, appointed in the place of Father Rodion." But he did not do this, and disappeared behind the eikonostasis by a side-door. He there bowed three times to the ground, and then bowed to Cyril, who was standing at the altar in his vestments, and stood some way off. During the whole of the mass he stood in the same place, and evinced genuine piety, whispered the prayers, and at suitable moments made profound bows, while at others, he only bowed his head ; and his face the whole time had a look of concentration in prayer. After the mass he came up to Cyril at the altar and respectfully received his blessing.

" Allow me to make myself known to you—I am Makárii Siloámski," said he.

Cyril introduced himself and invited

---

[1] The screen which divides off the place where the altar stands, from the rest of the church.

the new-comer to his house after church.

"Yes, yes, of course we must have a conversation about business," said Siloámski.

After mass he drank tea at Cyril's house. He appeared to be a cheery and talkative man, spoke about the seminary, about the teachers, the rector, and the inspector. He had only finished the course last summer, and had been the psalm-reader there for a whole year. Cyril remembered him as a small boy in the first class at the time that he left the seminary.

"I went to pay my respects to the bishop before I started, and he said many pleasant things about you. He said that you were very learned and that all ought to take example from you," said Siloámski, among other things.

"I am very much obliged to the bishop," replied Cyril.

"Well, I hope that we shall live in peace and concord," said the young priest, getting up to go.

"I hope so too." Cyril purposely refrained from all explanations—things would explain themselves.

That evening the Obnovliénskis paid a visit to the lady of the manor. This was Mura's first visit to her since the birth of her child. They were sitting in the dining-room drinking tea. The windows looking on to the garden were open. The lilac-trees were in flower and the room was filled with their aroma. Cyril related how he had made the new priest's acquaintance, and said he was glad the bishop had sent a young man, and that this was his first appointment. "He has never been corroded by routine, and love of gain. A young mind is easier won over to the right side, and you will see he will be an excellent colleague for me."

Nadiéshda Alecsiéëvna listened with a sceptical look. Her eyes, fixed on Cyril, seemed to say, "What a naïve and innocent child you are! Don't you trouble to look for a companion, because you won't find another like yourself!"

The servant at this moment informed Madame Kroupiéëv that the new clergyman had come; she decided to receive him in the next room, and went out.

The door was half-open, so that the conversation was audible in the room where the Obnovliénskis were sitting.

Siloámski entered sedately, and began to look for the holy image. Finding a small eikon in the corner near the ceiling, he crossed himself three times and bowed in front of it. He then bowed to his hostess.

"Allow me to make myself known to you: the newly-appointed priest, Makárii Siloámski."

Nadiéshda Alecsiéëvna bowed, and asked him to sit down. "Have you been here long?" said she, by way of opening a conversation.

"I only arrived yesterday, but I attended mass nevertheless this morning and made the acquaintance of my colleague, Father Cyril. I have lost no time in calling on you. Allow me most highly respected Nadiéshda Alecsiéëvna to count on your good favour."

"I am at your service."

"I am not going to trouble you with any requests now, but in the future I may want something: for example, if I get another cow, where am I to keep it? Or again, if I have not enough hay, where am I to get it, if not from the generous proprietress?"

"I am at your service," repeated Nadiéshda Alecsiéëvna, and got up with a colder look on her face than when they met.

"I will not trouble you any further now," said Father Makárii, also getting up and bowing his head, and putting his right hand on his breast.

Nadiéshda Alecsiéëvna inclined her head and said—"This way, if you please. This door leads into the garden. . . . You have got your own horses, I suppose?"

"Yes, I have a pair . . . I got them for my wife . . . they are very fair horses. . . . My respects to you!"

Nadiéshda Alecsiéëvna returned to the dining-room and began to talk about the gardener, who had been drunk for three days and had not appeared in the garden. She generally avoided speaking badly of people, considering this to be the business of gossips.

"Why don't you tell us anything about your visitor?" asked Mura.

"He produced an unfavourable impression on me," said Nadiéshda Alecsiéëvna, and returned to the subject of the gardener. Cyril sorrowfully bent down his head, and thought, "He has hardly shown himself before he begins to give notice, 'I am a person who will ask for all I want, bear that in mind!'

He wants nothing at present, but he does not wish it to be thought that he is an independent sort of person. What a strange thing it is! Where does this come from? They don't teach such things in the seminary, and he had had very little other experience besides the seminary. It must be in the blood, and descend from one generation to another. It is very, very melancholy."

The evening passed slowly. Nadiéshda Alecsiéëvna was under the influence of the bad impression created by her visitor. She tried in vain to entertain her guests. Cyril listened inattentively and answered without interest. He kept thinking about the peculiar inherited weaknesses of his brethren.

They returned home early, shortly after nine o'clock. Mura hurried to the child. As soon as they arrived they were astonished to find two visitors waiting for them at the front door. These were the deacon, Simeon, and the diatchók, Dementii. They were sitting on stools specially placed there for them by Feókla. At Cyril's arrival they both respectfully got up, holding their hats in their hands.

"Why are you sitting here, gentlemen? Why did you not wait in the room? Did you not ask them to come in, Feókla?"

"Yes, bátoushka, I asked them to come into the room, but they declined," answered Feókla.

"Oh, it's nothing! . . . It's so pleasant in the open air now," mildly observed the deacon.

Cyril invited them into the sitting-room. Mária Gavrilovna hurried into the bedroom to look after her son.

"Well, gentlemen, what is it?" said Cyril, as soon as his subordinates were seated.

The deacon coughed, and said, somewhat hesitatingly—"We have come to you, Father Cyril, about our business. I and Dementii Ermilitch have long determined to call your attention . . ."

The diatchók at this moment, evidently thinking that Father Simeon was making a mess of it, coughed loudly and interrupted—

"We are perishing, Father Cyril—we are simply perishing!"

Cyril glanced up at him. "What do you mean?" said he.

"We are dying of hunger."

"Of hunger?"

"Yes, Father Cyril. We hesitated a long while, and were afraid of disturbing you. . . . But at last there is nothing for it. . . . We have large families, and nothing to give them to eat. We may say that we ourselves are weak from hunger. . . . The lady of the manor's salary is perfectly inadequate; we have very little land; we are not allowed to take money from the people."

"Quite true, quite true," added the deacon.

"We don't ask for any superfluities, Father Cyril, but simply for bread to eat—for existence. Our children are crying; they want food."

Cyril walked about the room with his head bent down and his hands behind his back. It seemed to him now quite clear that the deacon and diatchók could not possibly live on their salaries.

His own salary was only just adequate to support life; and, besides, they had heaps of children, while he had only one, who as yet had cost him nothing. The position was complicated. He was the cause of their poverty and was powerless to help them. If he had anything left, he would gladly have offered it to them, but he had nothing. He could not possibly depart now from his newly-introduced principles. This had been his first victory, and he valued it highly.

"Father Cyril!" cautiously interrupted the deacon. Cyril stopped and looked at him. "We have come to you to make a request."

"Well, well?" hastily said Cyril. He heartily wished that this petition would be something which would satisfy their wants, and which he could grant.

"We have very little land, Father Cyril, but you have a good deal, and very good church land. You are doing nothing with it, so why not give it to us in return for a fourth part of its yield?"

"How much land have I got?" eagerly asked Cyril.

"Fifty dessyatines altogether, six of which is grass land."

"Well, that's first-rate! first-rate!" joyfully exclaimed Cyril. "You work it. I don't want anything for it. I don't understand these affairs, and besides, I've got enough. . . . Yes, yes, you take it."

Cyril's subordinates looked at each other in astonishment. "What does this mean?" Dementii began, but thought it better not to continue.

Cyril thought for a minute, and then

said—"Well, tell me, will this satisfy you?"

"We are very grateful—sincerely grateful," said they, bowing low.

"Well, now go, God be with you, and work the land, only don't be angry with me."

The deacon and diatchók again bowed and hastily went out.

"He is really a good fellow!" said the deacon, almost in Dementii's ear, when they had reached the church.

"We must begin work to-morrow at dawn. But what's the good of it?—he will probably change his mind. . . . Either the lady of the manor or Father Makárii will persuade him to alter his decision."

"It seems that Makárii is not one of his sort; he is a crafty fellow. . . . One can see that already. He appeared in church to show off his piety, and then flew straight off to the manor-house. He has already begun to beg for some favour."

"Well, anyhow *we* shall be all right now," said Dementii, with a joyful face, patting the deacon on the back, who bent like a twig under his heavy hand. "It's at the rate of twenty-five dessyatines apiece, and if we add our own fifteen, that makes forty dessyatines each! What? We are regular squires now, father deacon! He *is* a good fellow! It's a pity he's got something wrong in his head."

When Cyril entered the bedroom Mura asked him—

"Why did you do that, Cyril?"

"They are in a state of destitution, Mura," answered he.

"But you might have got six hundred roubles for the land."

"Oh! have you made this calculation?" asked Cyril, in a tone of genuine surprise.

"Feókla told me." mournfully answered Mura, and did not say any more about it. Feókla also, who had overheard the conversation, rattled the kitchen poker to express her dissatisfaction.

XII.

FATHER MAKÁRII SILO-AMSKI was one of those pupils at the seminary who, from childhood, devote their whole energies to the attainment of one fixed object—that is, to obtain a living. The living presents itself to their minds exclusively in the form of income, sacks of corn, measures of rye, willing offerings from the richer parishioners of fowls and chickens—both living and roasted, of fresh piquant aromatic "knish," of grain, with all possible kinds of exemptions and privileges, which it is every one's duty to confer on the pastor, and, generally speaking, a full measure of material comfort, with everything cut and dried for them. The services of the church—the mass, morning and evening service, and various ceremonies—form a sort of accessory to all this. But it never enters their head to think about the people that they are thrown amongst, or about their influence in the parish. When they have attained their wished-for aim, they become merely fulfillers of ceremonies. The parishioners demand their services, they go; and the parishioners fulfil their part of the contract and supply income. Their flocks look on them in the light of performers of the church services, and expect no spiritual instruction from them, except such as is conveyed through the services and ceremonies of the church.

Such seminary students as these confine their love of knowledge to elementary text-books. Their reading does not get beyond selections from classical authors in school manuals. In the department of theological study they, as a rule, get no further. Thus it is, that no external influence prevents them from carrying out their object in life, which is to prepare themselves for a living, for the sake of their own material welfare. When, therefore, they find themselves in the company of intelligent people they sometimes venture on such short and authoritative remarks as that "Gógol was a very clever writer," or that Tourgénief wrote "Biéjin loug," and that Póushkin wrote "Teliéga jízni." When they settle down in their parishes, they subscribe to the *Neva*[1] and the *Diocesan News*, which form their only bonds of communication with the intelligent world; and looking at them without prejudice, one is painfully impressed with their lack of intelligence, and one wonders what can they teach the unenlightened masses? With what light can they enlighten them? As years go on, they forget even the little that they learned from the school-books, and instead of raising their flocks to their own level, they gradually become like them, and imbibe all their prejudices and errors.

Father Makárii, during his time at the

---

[1] One of the Russian illustrated papers.

seminary, had taken part in the episcopal choir. He had a high tenor voice, and at one time, his worldly acquaintances had even advised him to take up the musical profession and become an opera singer. But he looked at things from a practical point of view, and did not pine for fame, and considered that a bird in the hand—that is the parish—was worth two in the bush. In recognition of his services in the choir, the bishop appointed him to Lúgovoë, as Lúgovoë had the reputation of being an excellent parish. So he bought Father Rodion's house through an agent, and started off for Lúgovoë with his head full of dreams of the wealth of the parish. After he had conducted his first funeral, he was very much disturbed at receiving nothing. It seemed to him awkward at the very outset of his career, to demand money straight from the moujik. So he turned round to Dementii—

"What about payment? How do you generally arrange it—before or after?"

"They give nothing," said Dementii, looking at the deacon with a very sly air, as much as to say, "See what an ugly face he will make in a minute!"

But Siloámski made no face, and simply stared, almost angrily, at Dementii.

"I did not ask as a joke," said he; "I want to know what the custom is here."

Dementii again looked expressively at the deacon, and seemed to say, "Watch him well, father deacon, watch him well."

"The custom here is not to take a single copeck for services performed. Everything is done gratis. We only take the *pain béni* after the requiem mass, &c."

"It seems you are trying to make a fool of me!" said Siloámski, with his former angry tone, which, at the same time, betrayed a shade of anxiety.

"How could I do such a thing? I would not dare to joke with you; the father deacon will confirm all I say."

"It is perfectly true," rejoined the latter. "Up to Father Cyril's time there were incomes, and very good ones too, but Father Cyril abolished them."

"What do you mean, abolished them? One has got to live somehow! I . . . simply don't understand it."

"Wait a bit, my friend, you'll understand soon enough," thought Dementii, and added—

"Certainly you must live, and you must live on your salary! The lady of the manor has appointed a salary to each one of us: the priests receive fifty roubles a month each, and we get considerably less!"

Siloámski mechanically lifted a coloured handkerchief to his brow to wipe off the perspiration. He felt just as if he had suddenly tumbled into a trap.

"Oh! that's the arrangement, is it? A parish without income! Ha, ha! We will see, we will see! . . . It is necessary to find out by what right the chief arranges matters thus! We will see!"

He said this in undisguised anger, and, forgetting about the propriety of preserving a pious air, pulled off his vestments with such energy, that it might have been imagined he wanted to tear them to pieces.

Dementii and the deacon were mightily pleased. They did not like Siloámski, and they took pleasure in referring to the former incomes, to add to the anguish of his heart. They themselves were perfectly happy now. On Cyril's land, which they had divided between them, the first green blades of the hoped-for crops were appearing, and they considered themselves regular squires.

Siloámski went home first, but then rushed out of the room, and flew off to Cyril. Entering the chief's house, he even forgot to say "How do you do?" and at once began about business in his high tenor voice.

"Excuse me, Father Cyril! What is the meaning of this? By what right have you altered the customs here? By what right have you introduced such arrangements?"

"What's it all about? What are you talking about?" asked Cyril, getting up from the dinner-table and wiping his mouth with his napkin. Mária Gavrílovna looked at him in alarm.

"I simply ask you by what right you do such things? Where is such a law? Show me this law!" continued Siloámski, perfectly maddened by his disillusionment with regard to the "best parish for income." "Although you are chief, you have no such rights! Excuse me, you have no such rights!"

"Please explain yourself, Father Makárii, I understand nothing."

"Why you have abolished the legal incomes, and have introduced some sort of salaries . . . some fifty roubles a month, I believe. . . . I am very much obliged to you, but all the same I have a right to my legal income."

"Yes," said Cyril, firmly, "that is our custom, and you must make the best of it."

"Not if I know it! What!—acquiesce in these customs which you have introduced? Never! I refuse your salary, and shall demand my rights. What right have you? You exceed your rights! I shall complain, and you . . you will be sent to the monastery. . . . Don't imagine that because you are a 'magistrant,' you can do just as you like! The bishop is my friend, I was in his choir. . . . So take care!"

"Although I was never a singer, I must beg you to leave my house, as you do not know how to behave properly!" said Cyril, hiding his vexation with difficulty. Here was a young pastor, who had scarcely entered on his duties, who already demanded money so persistently and angrily—who demanded the right to turn his vocation into a trade! This maddened him, and vexed and grieved him most profoundly. And he had counted on his youth, which, as he had imagined, could not have been hardened by custom. Father Rodion was an old man and infused with old ideas, and even he had not insisted so determinedly on his right to income.

When Siloámski heard this request to leave the chief's house, made in a very stern way, his wrath suddenly cooled down. He had not wished to insult the chief, and did not even wish to quarrel with him. Such a course of action was contrary to his principles. But in his outburst of indignation he forgot that he was speaking too loud and generally misbehaving himself.

"Pardon me," said he to Mária Gavrílovna, and bowed to her; "in my impulse I really . . . went too far, and perhaps said something insulting. Allow me to explain."

But Cyril was no longer listening to him. He was walking about the room in great agitation. His peace was again disturbed. For more than six months he had been alone in the parish, and he had begun to think that the new institutions founded by him had taken permanent root, and had become a law about which there could be no question. But he was chiefly vexed that this young man understood him as little and even less than Father Rodion. Did this mean that he was ever to wage war, alone in the field? Was it possible that this traditional atmosphere, amidst which the new generation of pastors was educated, had so entirely invaded and permeated them, that their minds were perfectly inaccessible to more enlightened ideas, and that they were absolutely incapable of grasping the nature of the problems before them? What were their problems? Merely those that were common to all mankind—namely, to live for their pleasure, and to provide for their old age.

Cyril stopped and looked sadly at Siloámski. He said in a low and weary tone, "What is the use of explanations, Father Makárii? It is perfectly clear that we cannot understand one another. You and I are absolutely different—the gulf between us is too great! We have different ideas, different objects, and different tendencies. You want income, and I do not: to you income is a pleasure, to me it is an insult! You have come here to provide for yourself, and I to serve the poor and ignorant. How are we ever to understand each other? I will tell you this: you may do what you like, but the customs which I have introduced I will never give up. That is all I have to tell you."

Cyril sat down on the sofa, pale, and thoroughly unnerved. Siloámski looked at him from under his eyebrows, then looked at Mária Gavrilovna in the same way, took up his hat, turned to the door and went out.

For a week Siloámski remained in a sulky state and undertook no business. After Cyril's tirade, he felt that the decision expressed by him to claim his rights at all hazards was considerably weakened. He understood that this was not mere obstinacy on Cyril's part, and, strangely enough, he attributed it, just as Father Rodion had done, to madness.

A week passed. One evening Siloámski invited the deacon Simeon to come and drink tea with him and the mátoushka. The latter was a very young and pretty blonde; she had a sonorous voice. "You know, father deacon, this is dreadful—simply dreadful!" said she to the deacon, in a lisping tone, and her bright eyes looking as though they were just going to cry. "We have spent money, bought this house, and suddenly ... I can hardly believe that the authorities will allow such arbitrary proceedings."

"Yes, we must make the best of it!

I and Dementii Ermilitch have suffered for a whole year!" said the deacon, with false sympathy, forgetting of course about Cyril's land.

"But tell me, if you please, father deacon, what sort of person is the lady of the manor?" asked Siloámski.

"The lady of the manor? The Lord only knows what sort of person she is. We never see her. She sits in her garden like a bear in a hole. She mixes with no one, and avoids the clergy."

"H'm! That's suspicious."

"She is on very good terms with Father Cyril; they often visit one another."

"Oh! . . . that's very suspicious . . . very! I shall go to the bishop and inform him of this."

"To the bishop? I wouldn't advise you to."

"Why? The bishop is very fond of me. I used to sing in his choir."

"Yes, it's perfectly true. He even used to render the solos sometimes," said the mátoushka, not without a certain amount of pride.

"All the same I would not advise you to go to him," said the deacon.

"But why? tell me, please. He is acting in a perfectly illegal manner."

"I allow it. But Father Rodion said the same thing, and went to the bishop, but the affair turned out badly. The bishop said to him, 'I set up this priest, that is Father Cyril, as an example to the whole diocese, and approve of all his doings!' That is the bishop's opinion. And when Father Rodion hinted about his being transferred to another place, the bishop said, 'I have no cause for punishing him, but if you like it I will transfer you'—that is Father Rodion—and he transferred him. Such are the opinions of the lord bishop!"

"Perhaps so," replied Siloámski, with assurance. "But Father Rodion and I are quite different people."

"Certainly!" interrupted the mátoushka. "I have already told you that he even sang the solos. It's not every one that can do that!"

To put matters shortly, Siloámski resolved to follow Father Rodion's example and go to the bishop. He started off in company with his wife, who was a native of the town.

After Father Rodion's trip to the government town, reports about the young priest had become current, as to how the young "magistrant" Obnovliénski had taken a country parish, and had established a new order of things, and declined to take money from the people. But these reports had not made much impression. No one thoroughly believed them. Father Rodion had told two or three of his friends in his outburst of dissatisfaction, but after his conversation with the bishop he had said no more about it.

Siloámski looked up all his numerous acquaintances in the town. Father Makárii visited the bátoushkas and his spouse called on their wives. Siloámski even went to the rector of the seminary, Father Mejof, and told him about Cyril.

"Yes, yes, it's just as I foresaw, and I warned the bishop of it. Even when he left here for the academy, there was something strange and presumptuous in his character."

"He was always a bit cracked, but now he is quite mad!" remarked young Mejof, who was present at this interview, and who at the present time was very successfully fulfilling the post of inspector of the seminary. "What right has a 'magistrant' to bury himself in the country? There is not an atom of sense in it!"

"I tell you what, Siloámski," proposed the rector—"don't you rush off to the bishop. I will go to him first and talk to him seriously. We must put all our forces together to bring this young man to his senses! Or, better still, you be at the bishop's at ten o'clock to-morrow morning, and I will meet you there."

Reports of Cyril's eccentricities soon reached the houses of the clergy in the government town, and towards evening Father Gávriil Fortificantof and his wife heard of them.

"Whatever are we to do?" exclaimed Nikoláevna. "He has succeeded in getting himself talked about in the town and in the whole government. And this is my son-in-law, the husband of my daughter! This cannot go on! Father Gávriil, you must take steps to remedy this; you must go to the bishop's, and beg, demand, I don't know what! . . . You must save my daughter!"

Father Gávriil was a man of a calm disposition, and always acted on the maxim that every evil rights itself in the end; nevertheless, in consequence of his wife's persistent demands, he started off to the rector to consult him. They arranged to go together to the bishop.

Arriving at the episcopal palace the following day, they found his lordship's carriage standing at the door, harnessed with four black horses. They hastened upstairs. The rector took the lead, walking with an air of great importance, Siloámski followed him, ascending the stairs very briskly, and at some distance followed Father Gávriil, with his head bent down and moving slowly. The bishop came to them at once. He was dressed in a dark green cassock, and in a long mantle with a hood to it. In his right hand he held a thick walking-stick with a handsome top, and in the left hand the rosary, but not the black ones hung on a silk thread, which he usually had in his hands, but one used on state occasions made of rare and beautiful stones. He was evidently starting off somewhere.

"Ah! what an honourable triumvirate!" said he, in a joking tone. "I can guess already what you have come about! You, singer, have come to complain of Cyril Obnovliénski, haven't you? I can see it by your eyes. And the father rector wants to support you with his authority! and as for you, Father Gávriil, I can only suppose that you have come for the sake of good company! Well, what is it? Speak! Who is going to speak?"

"Your lordship has guessed aright," ventured Siloámski.

"I thought so—I thought as much! I guessed it at once! And what's your complaint? No income? Eh?"

"I consider it my duty to say that for my part . . ." began the rector, with importance; but the bishop would not let him go on.

"You should be ashamed of yourselves, my friends, you should!" said he, decisively. "We ought to rejoice at such an apparition as this young priest—and you come with a complaint! He has refused the advantages of a town living, he has declined honours, and disinterestedly serves those around him. What is there bad in that? You, father rector, you are a famous dogmatist: tell me, is there anything essentially bad in his action?"

"But, your Reverence, his relations with the lady of the place, Madame Kroupićëv are suspicious!" hastily said Siloámski, as though fearing that the bishop would interrupt him at the first word.

At this statement the rector's face assumed an expression of surprise, and Father Gávriil got red from vexation.

"You foolish fellow!" sternly said the bishop; "for such a lie I ought to send you to the monastery for a month! There is nothing suspicious in his doings—his mind is as pure as a child's." With these words the bishop went out. The triumvirate stood where they were, distressed by the unexpected turn affairs had taken. When they descended to the courtyard the carriage had gone; they all three went away in different directions, and Siloámski disappeared in an unknown direction very quickly: he had an unpleasant impression that the effect of his exclamation about the lady of the manor had been to spoil the whole affair.

After this episode the relations between the clergy at Lúgovoë became more peaceful. Siloámski returned from the town and pretended that nothing special had occurred. Neither he nor his wife said a word to any one about the interview with the bishop. When the deacon, who took a keen interest in the progress of events, asked Siloámski one day what the bishop had said, the latter answered in a calm and innocent sort of way, "Oh, you know, I changed my mind, and did not go to him after all. It is awkward, you know, to speak ill of one's companions—it would be almost like slander. No, I have decided to stay on here a little and then simply ask to be transferred somewhere else, without explaining the reason."

Siloámski was wonderfully polite and respectful to Cyril: he never raised his voice, and by way of extra courtesy sent his wife to call on Mura. They talked together for a quarter of an hour, and Madame Siloámski carefully observed the most perfect politeness. Mura returned the visit, and here their acquaintance ended.

At length Siloámski could stand it no longer. He received no income, and neither managed to cultivate or let his church land; he looked upon a further stay in Lúgovoë as so much loss of time. So he again visited the town, brought all his influence to bear among his musical friends, and got transferred to another place. In July Father Rodion's house was empty, and Cyril, to his great delight, again found himself alone in the parish.

XIII.

ON the meanwhile the inhabitants of Lúgovoë, and of the whole district, were being threatened with a famine. Scarcely a drop of rain had fallen during the whole of May and June. The rye, which had attained about half its growth, turned prematurely yellow and produced a miserable ear without any grain in it. The rye failed everywhere in the district, and they mowed it for the sake of the straw. There was still a hope that rain would fall towards St. John the Baptist's Day, and that the wheat might be saved; but this hope was not fulfilled, and the half-grown wheat crop faded away, without even showing signs of an ear. The steppe for ten versts around, presented the sad spectacle of yellow pasture land and black fields. The cattle wandered sadly over the dried-up pasture, and, exhausted by hunger and by the insupportable scorching heat, stood in the bare fields looking for whole hours at the blue sky, which showed no sign of the smallest cloud. At times the whole herd seemed to be seized with a sort of sudden impulse, and, trampling with their hoofs on the dried-up earth, they rushed down to the meadow streamlet, but instead of water they saw the winding narrow bed, long since dried up, and expressed their grief with heart-rending lowing. The water from the wells was preserved as carefully as gold. They gave the cattle water in handfuls, fearing that the supply would dry up and that they would die from thirst. The villagers had a supply of grain from last year which they dealt out very carefully. However, their hopes were not yet quite exhausted. The rye had failed—they had placed their hopes on the wheat; the wheat began to turn yellow—then they relied on the millet. But at length July drew to an end, and St. Elijah's Day passed without rain, and when August arrived all hopes were at an end.

Cyril found gloomy faces everywhere, both in church and on his visits among the people, and he himself became gloomier every day. Going past the public-house he heard shouting, singing, and abusive language, and the thought struck him that, during better times, this shouting was not so often heard, and was less noisy. It seemed to him strange that these unenlightened country people, even in the days of famine, managed to find something to spend on drink. He stopped, admonished, and tried to bring them to reason.

"What difference does it make, bátoushka?" answered one of them, considerably under the influence of *vodka*. "We have got to die of hunger, and it's better to die in a jovial frame of mind."

"It's not necessary to die; you must

struggle against the famine," said Cyril; but he seemed to feel himself that these were mere empty words because the struggle was an impossible one. He thought to himself, " It's not a case of struggling, but of bearing the evil patiently in the hope of things taking a turn for the better."

Cases of cattle plague occurred in the middle of August. The cattle died from exhaustion and thirst, and fell down dead in the fields. Lamentations were heard in various parts of the village.

" It will soon be with us as with the cattle!" said the moujiks, looking at a dead cow and weeping as if they had lost their nearest relation.

Cyril returned home exhausted and gloomy. Unpleasant thoughts crowded into his head. He saw before him perfectly helpless people threatened by famine. He had spoken consoling words, but recognized with a heavy heart that words in such a case are of no use, and that help was required in the form of bread. A sort of indecision seized him. There were moments when all his practical work, on which he had laid so great a stress, seemed a mere empty amusement, and nothing more. What had he really done? He had taught, he had enlightened, and perhaps he had made a few people wiser, or instructed some erring soul, but now, when it was a question of preserving the health and even the life of the people, he was powerless. He had put a stop to taking money from the people, but that was no advantage to them now, as they had none to give.

One day, when he was dining with

Mura, a boy, in a dirty, worn-out shirt, with bare feet, with a pale face, spotted with patches, came to inform Cyril that his mother had died.

"What did she die of?" asked Cyril, in a tone betraying emotion. Three days before, he had seen the boy's mother tottering under the weight of pails of water which she was carrying from the well.

"The Lord knows!" said the boy, stupidly gazing into space. "From food, I suppose."

"What do you mean, 'from food'?" continued Cyril, with still greater anxiety, and with a presentiment of evil in his mind.

"She made some porridge out of the siftings, and it finished her off."

"The siftings—that means bran!" explained Cyril to Mura, in a very low voice. "It has come to this, that they have to eat bran."

He walked about the room almost deliriously. A terrible storm awoke in his breast. He felt as though some unknown force drove and urged him on to action, and that he had ceased to belong to himself. Mura looked at him with alarm and wonder. She quietly said to the boy—"Go, the bátoushka will follow!" and when the boy had gone out, she asked—"Cyril, what is the matter with you?" She got up and went to him. His face was pale; his large eyes sparkled as though he had a fever. She took his hand; he stopped. "What is the matter with you, Cyril?" repeated Mura, in a trembling tone.

"Ah, Mura!" and his head sank on her breast.

Mura felt that he was weeping, and tried to calm him, although she could not understand the cause of his grief.

"What! you don't understand? A famine is beginning; this is the first death from hunger. A mortal famine, Mura, is beginning, not far from busy towns where commerce goes on in its usual way and people amuse themselves and provide themselves with superfluities! This is terrible, Mura! One cannot stand by and look on with one's arms folded. How can we eat our dinner when a poor woman dies from eating bran. . . . It's impossible! . . . We must do something active."

This he said in a halting voice, and looking out of the window at the village. He imagined to himself that death had already begun to visit every hut, and that he was too late with his help. Anyhow, he was too late to help this woman who had died from eating bran.

"But what can we do, Cyril? We are in a state of destitution ourselves," said Mura. Cyril did not answer her. He hastily put on his cassock, seized his hat and ran out of the room. He almost ran along the road to the manor-house. The wind blew around the skirts of his cassock and filled the long sleeves, and as he strode along waving his arms, he resembled some huge bird flying very low over the land.

"Where is our bátoushka rushing off to?" asked the moujiks, among themselves, in surprise; "something must have happened. See how pale he is, and how his eyes glitter!"

Cyril scarcely noticed how he got

over the three versts. He impulsively opened the garden gate, and walked up to the house without taking any notice of the furious barking of a chained dog, who, although he frequently saw Cyril, could never get accustomed to his cassock. He ascended the steps leading to the front door and went into the vestibule. There he met a housemaid.

"Where is Nadiéshda Alecsiéëvna?" asked he; and not waiting for an answer, entered the dining-room.

Nadiéshda Alecsiéëvna had only just sat down to dinner. The small boy sat next to her on a high chair with a napkin tied round his neck. Seeing Cyril, she put down the soup-ladle and got up. His expression was so extraordinary that she did not even think of asking him if he would dine with her, but said—

"What has happened? Tell me, quickly! Is anything the matter with Mária Gavrilovna or the child?"

"No, no! It's the famine—people are dying of hunger!" answered he, with an increasingly loud voice, and pointing in the direction of the village—"There!" added he.

The tone of his voice and his movements were majestic. As though inspired with a command, he could not speak in an ordinary way at that moment, he could only summon, arouse, and preach. Those words which he had just uttered would have seemed to him half an hour before bombastic, and that grandiose gesture, theatrical.

"Where?" asked Nadiéshda Alecsiéëvna. She knew that the crops had failed, and that her own farming operations had suffered, although not in the same degree, because she had a great deal of land and on some parts of her property things had turned out better. But she had no idea that it was a case of famine.

"In the village," answered Cyril, in the same tone as before. "They are beginning to come to me to bury the dead; a woman has already died from eating bran. That means that there is absolutely nothing to eat. And you and I eat plentiful dinners and have all the comforts of life. Listen, Nadiéshda Alecsiéëvna—I will give up everything I possess, to the very last crumb. Substantial help is required! You can help—you ought to help—you ought to—and you will! I know you have a kind heart."

In ordinary moments he would never have brought himself to say this to her. He would have considered it importunate and meddlesome on his part, and, although the request was for others, he would have thought it quite inexcusable. But at such a time he could not trouble himself with the exigencies of politeness. He looked straight at the matter and saw one fact —a terrible death from hunger. His pale face expressed stern command, and his ardent look penetrated Nadiéshda Alecsiéëvna's spirit. She now saw before her, not the meek and mild clergyman, who at times hesitated even to utter his opinions, and when he became excited, evidently tried to stifle his feelings and speak quietly. Before her now stood an inspired prophet, in long biblical attire, with the pale face of an ascetic, with the expression of a deeply suffering martyr."

She was greatly agitated by his speech, looks, and manners. She, too, felt as though carried away by impulse, and as though seized by a desire to aid him in the work of charity.

In such a frame of mind she warmly grasped his hand, and then quickly disappeared into another room.

In a couple of minutes she returned went up to Cyril, and handed him a small bundle of bank-notes.

"Here is a small sum," said she, in a trembling voice; "about three hundred roubles. But I have more in the town. ... I can get it! ... Excuse me," added she, putting her hand to her forehead, as though she had a sudden idea, "I must speak to the bailiff. Call the bailiff!"

He was an old man with a long beard, and intelligent, penetrating eyes, who had served during Madame Kroupiéëv's father's lifetime, and had begun life as a serf. He had held this post both under young Kroupiéëv, and also under the disorderly, drunken *régime* of Madame Kroupiéëv's cousin, and now had the management of the whole property.

"How much corn have we got?" asked Nadiéshda Alecsiéëvna, when he came in.

"Only what remains over from last year," answered the latter. "If you want to sell it, it is not worth the trouble of scraping up: about one hundred pouds [1] of wheat and about forty quarters of

---

[1] Poud=thirty-six pounds.

other grain. There are about thirty pouds of barley, but we shall want it ourselves; and considering that the crops have failed this summer it will not even be sufficient.

"Very well, you can go."

But the bailiff hesitated, evidently wishing to say something.

"If you please, there are four moujiks who want a measure of corn each; they say that if you don't give it, they will die of hunger."

"Give it to them at once—this minute."

"Very well."

The bailiff went out.

"Now let us come along," said Cyril.

"I am quite ready," answered she, and having hastily made arrangements for her son being looked after, they started off. They both thought that they ought to go on foot, because to drive in a carriage at a moment when hunger and death were about, would be almost insulting to the people. The parishioners again gazed with astonishment when they saw Madame Kroupiéév and Cyril hurrying into the village with agitated and alarmed expressions on their faces. They walked in silence, and Nadiéshda Alecsiéëvna hardly managed to keep pace with Cyril.

This poor woman's death was only a prelude to the misfortunes which were threatening Lúgovoë. She had died more or less accidentally, because, overcome by hunger, she had eaten too much of this chaffy food. But famine was now torturing the inhabitants of half the huts in the large village. Their inmates had absolutely no bread, and there remained only a small quantity of bran from last year's crops which had not been eaten by the pigs. In some of the huts the inhabitants had killed their cattle, but these unfortunate creatures were so thin and enervated that they hardly supplied any food to their owners. The children were playing listlessly in the yards, they were pale, and their stomachs protruded. Cyril and Nadiéshda Alecsićëvna began their visits at the first hut, and at every step their despair increased. They found suffering people in almost every hut who laid on couches near the stoves, and their friends were too feeble to help them. The moujiks tried to go to work, but as the whole district was in a state of famine they had not sufficient strength to walk to places where they might have found employment. Besides this, the price of labour had fallen so low that it would not have been worth it. It was clear that they must have been suffering from hunger some weeks already, and that the effects of it were now beginning to be felt.

"Why did you not tell me? Why did not one come to me for help?" asked Nadiéshda Alecsićëvna.

To this they answered nothing, and it seemed to her that even now they accepted her help unwillingly and suspiciously. "I suppose if I had not been with the clergyman, they would not even have admitted me into their huts," thought she; and it seemed to her perfectly natural and comprehensible. How many years had she lived here side by side with these people without interesting herself about their thoughts or lives! She had shut herself up, and devoted herself entirely to her son, feeling a sort of contempt for all people. It was not these people who had awakened contempt in her, but others, and so it had happened that she had avoided these also, and they only used to see her on rare occasions in church, and then she used to hurry home and shut herself up again in her half-ruined manor-house, surrounded by the garden. She was now paying for her neglect of the people by incurring their distrust.

They continued their visits till late at night, and then returned, tired out, to the church-house. Mura was in a great state of alarm. She could not think what had become of Cyril, and had imagined all sorts of dreadful things to herself.

"Ah! if only you could see what a terrible state they are in," exclaimed he, "you would have left everything, and come with us! They are hungry and ill, and have no one to help them. What a terrible thing it is to be far from help! So long as things go on well, they manage to make shift from day to day without requiring anything, but the moment misfortune comes, they are as helpless as if they were on an island in the middle of the ocean? Good Lord! How many people in the cities and towns there are who are full of intellect, intelligence, and heart, but without occupation—without even senseless occupation! Why don't they come here to this dark corner? Here living work is awaiting them eagerly! How cruel it is! Truly—*homo homini lupus est*. These grasping shopkeepers at once profit by the famine to put up the price of provisions to absurd prices. It is just the same in the time of war! It is terrible!"

"It is very sad," said Mura, with real sympathy; "but what can we do?—we have nothing ourselves."

Cyril remained silent, with his brows knitted. Nadiéshda Alecsiéëvna was thoughtfully looking out of the window. The thought struck her, what a strange couple these two were, and how little they had in common. He, a passionate enthusiast, idealist, who carried his ideas almost to fanaticism, and ready to forget everything else on earth for the sake of them; she, an ordinary sort of creature, who looked with astonishment on any new idea or any action out of the ordinary course of things. She did not understand him in the least, and he paid so little attention to his domestic surroundings that clearly, up to this time, he had not noticed this.

Cyril sat down at the writing-table. He wrote to all the authorities in the government town, drawing a gloomy picture of the state of affairs at Lúgovoë in the most energetic language: he asked for doctors, medicines, and food. . . . He then composed an appeal to be put in the newspapers, asking the citizens for help. Having done all this, he dispatched the sexton to the town on one of Madame Kroupiéev's best horses. He then went out again into the village. It was now three o'clock in the morning. All were asleep. Nadiéshda Alecsiéëvna sent for her carriage, returned to the manor-house, and having ascertained that her son was all right, came back again to the village. For two days they worked hard. They distributed, where necessary, both money and food, but devoted most of their attention to the numerous sick. They tried in vain to gauge the nature of the prevalent illness. The symptoms were fever and delirium, and Cyril thought it must be typhus fever, but, as he did not know the symptoms, had no real ground for his supposition. There were four funerals during these two days. On the third day the wife of a clerk living in the neighbourhood volunteered her services. She was about forty years old and pitted with small-pox, but a good-natured person. She had acted as a sister of mercy in the Turkish campaign, and was therefore acquainted more or less with medical matters. She set to work to rub the patients, to give them poultices, and even administered medicine. However, on the same day a doctor arrived from the town, and this was the whole extent of the help received from that quarter.

XIV.

MÁRIA GAVRILOVNA passed whole days in tears. Cyril had deserted her. He only returned home two or three times a day, spoke a few words to her, and went out again. A dozen times Mura had wished to speak to him, but without success. One day, however, she compelled him to listen to her.

"Cyril, what are you doing? what are you doing?" asked she, with a handkerchief in her hands, as tears were appearing every minute in her eyes.

Cyril looked at her vaguely, as though not understanding her question.

"Look at yourself in the glass. See what you are coming to. All your looks have gone. You will get ill and die."

"Nonsense, Mura! one ought not to think about such things. This is my duty, and I am only fulfilling it."

"You consider this your duty! You forget that you have a wife and child!"

"Yes, Mura, you are right. There are moments, and even hours, when I forget it. And how can I remember it when I see before me so much grief and suffering?" thoughtfully added Cyril.

"You cannot alleviate all the sufferings or console all the grief."

"Do not speak in that way, Mura, I beg you; this is the way people speak who do not wish to alleviate any suffering or console any grief. If you cannot alleviate all the suffering, you can at any rate do your best to alleviate that which we see before us. But whence did you get these cursed ideas of worldly prudence which stifle the voice of your heart? If you but knew, Mura, how painful it is for me to hear such sentiments from you. . . . Remember you are my wife, and that we are bound together inseparably. What! you seize me by the coat and wish to keep me at home when I should be busy with the sacred work of compassion and sympathy? I am young now; it is now only, during these years, that a man willingly gives himself up to noble impulses, and is ready to sacrifice his own material comfort. The ripe years of quiet rest will come, when we shall get to look indifferently at everything, except our own little nest. Why hurry on that day, Mura?"

"I don't understand you, Cyril; the only thing that is clear to me is that you no longer love me. You love all the world more than me and my son."

"Nonsense, Mura! It is true that I love all men, but you and Gavrousha I love specially. I cannot act otherwise than I am doing now. . . . No, Mura," said he, with an outburst of heartiness and almost joyfully, going up to her, taking her hand, and kissing her forehead; "do not ask me not to leave you. You are well and our son is well, and do not require my special care at this moment; whereas, there, if only you knew, if only you could see, how much I am wanted!"

He went out, and Mura again began to cry. And then Feókla came in to console her.

"I cannot understand what he is about!" exclaimed she, wiping her tears. "Every time I look at you, mátoushka, I think to myself how unfortunate you are. You have not even enough money to buy proper food . . . eggs or cream, just as though you were a nun."

Mura, in fact, at this time had a very scanty diet. Cyril had divided his last month's salary among the parishioners, and they had made shift on such food as Feókla had procured on credit from the shop. Feókla continued—

"Day and night, all alone with the baby, as though you were a widow; and he, your dear husband, our bátoushka, is with that 'panna.'[1] . . . The Lord alone knows him."

Mura looked out of the window to hide her face from Feókla. These last words tore her heart, and she sobbed loudly. From the window she saw Cyril walking down the village road to meet a small fat man, whom she recognized as the doctor sent from the town, and a few minutes later a carriage overtook them, in which Nadiéshda Alecsiéëvna was seated. Cyril and the doctor got into the carriage, and they started off to the other end of the village. Mura turned away from the window. Whether this was mere derangement of

---

[1] "Pan," the Polish word for lord, seigneur, squire; "panna"=lady. The word is also used in Little Russia and in the western provinces.

the nerves, or the effect of Feókla's hints, she could not tell, but at that moment she felt a dislike for Nadiéshda Alecsiéëvna.

An indistinct noise near the church railings at that moment made her tremble. She wiped her tears and ran down to the entrance. When she saw a carriage driving up to the house her breath failed her, and her heart beat fast. A minute later she was lying senseless in the arms of her mother, Anna Nikoláevna, and the old deacon Obnovliénski was supporting her with his arms.

They carried Mura into the room and laid her down on the sofa, where she remained unconscious. While they were preparing means to bring her round, Feókla, in a whisper, explained to them the position of affairs.

"You wouldn't believe it, my dear mátoushka! It's impossible to understand how she suffers! Day after day she is left alone with the baby; she has not even enough to eat; and all the time Father Cyril is in the peasants' huts with the panna."

She related everything down to the smallest details. The old deacon listened with his head bent down, as though guilty of his son's shortcomings. They had summoned him from Ustimiévka and brought him to Lúgovoë, in order that he should bring his parental influence to bear on his son. Although he perfectly well knew that his remonstrances would be in vain, he nevertheless dared not disobey the commands of the dignitary's wife, and had started off with her.

"I did not expect to find anything good here," said Mura's mother, with tears in her eyes, "but such things from your son I could never have believed possible."

The deacon continued to sit there with his head cast down and his hands on his knees. He knew quite well what his son would say to him. He would say, "This, bátoushka, is only what the gospel commands me to do; I am the Samaritan who takes the sick under his care and heals their wounds," and the old man would have nothing to answer to such an argument.

Mura regained consciousness and got up from the sofa. She was at first silent when her mother questioned her, but then told her all. Anna Nikoláevna told her straight that she would stand his nonsense no longer, but would teach him a lesson which he would remember. She ordered Mura to pack up her baggage at once. Feókla thoroughly approved of this measure and helped her to pack.

"That's it, my dear mátoushka; you may be sure that this will bring him to his senses," said she.

Mura was frightened by such a decisive step, and was for putting it off a bit, but her mother was inflexible.

"If he really loves you and your son, you may be sure that he will soon come after you; and if he does not love you—the devil take him!" added she, decisively, and the deacon who heard this, could not stand such an expression, and went out of the room. He went into the village to look for his son, to warn him of the impending evil. In the meanwhile

Mura's traps were all packed up, and she started off, weeping copious tears, with her mother and son, for the town.

The doctor had defined the prevalent illness in Lúgovoë as typhus fever. He was a short, jovial man, fat and broad-shouldered. He walked about with short but very resolute steps, and at each step moved forward one of his shoulders. His face was red, and he wore a short, square-cut, light-coloured beard with a reddish tinge. He had a turned-up nose, large grey eyes, and the thick hair on his head was close-cropped and stood on end. He was dressed in a grey canvas suit with a canvas cap.

He set to work energetically, and at once treated Cyril and Madame Kroupiéëv as though they were old friends. His name was Arkadii Andréëvitch Sapóshkof.

"You should rest a bit, madam, otherwise you will be pouring the medicine into their ears instead of their mouths," said he, to Nadiéshda Alecsiéëvna.

This was rather an exaggeration. Nadiéshda Alecsiéëvna had fulfilled the duties of sister of mercy very zealously, but on the day when the doctor arrived she was terribly worn out with sleeplessness and had not closed her eyes for two days.

He told Cyril that she would make a splendid nurse, and praised the clerk's wife for her skill, but earnestly requested her not to apply mustard plasters. There was one great disadvantage about him: at every moment he employed the most violent and abusive language.

"Why do you do that?" shortly asked Cyril, "can't you get on without it?"

"I know it is a senseless habit, bátoushka—" perfectly senseless!" answered he. "For instance, I am a fairly skilful physician; you see people are getting better. But take away from me the right to express my feelings, and I swear to you on my honour all my skill would go to the devil! It helps, you know, it helps wonderfully. I must tell you, bátoushka, that ten years ago, when I was a youngster in the military hospital during the war, I picked up the habit." He added that the presence of women always deterred him from this, and that he then had to content himself with biting his tongue. "But you, bátoushka, surprise me," said he to Cyril. "I've seen a good few bátoushkas in my life, old and young, important and modest. But under such circumstances they all shut themselves up in their cages—they are fearfully afraid of infection. But you, you are a brave bátoushka!"

Sapóshkof worked indefatigably, and succeeded in visibly diminishing the epidemic. This was easier as now in every hut they had bread to eat instead of bran. When Sapóshkof heard that the dealers had put up the price of bread, he ran off to the bazaar, in which were several shops kept by Jews.[1] Arrived here he assumed the tone of an important functionary, and made a tremendous commotion.

"Ah, you animals!" cried he, stamping about with his feet. "Do you know what I can do with you? I can have you

---

[1] The scene of this story being laid in Little Russia, it comes within the pale of Jewish settlement.

all locked up if you don't sell your bread at a reasonable price. I can order a detachment of soldiers at once from the town! Do you understand?"

To further impress them with his powers, he added several very forcible words. The dealers got frightened and brought their prices down to the normal figure. This young doctor acted generally in a very determined manner. He saw that he had not enough volunteers, and that they were not strong enough to get through all that there was to be done. They were only three in all, and his regular patients amounted to thirty. So he collected some old women, brought them to the patients, and made them act as sick nurses, and if they showed fear, or unwillingness, he said—

"It doesn't matter, you are not worth the air you breathe. What! are you afraid of infection? Are you afraid of dying? How very sad! It's all right; you will die, you will be buried, the worms will eat you—that's all! Hurry up! Don't lose time."

The moujiks were delighted with him, and were especially pleased by his choice selection of language.

"I assure you many of them recovered from that alone!" said he to Cyril; "they hear a familiar word, and their spirits rejoice and revive."

The deacon Obnovliénski found Cyril, with the help of a peasant, at the other end of the village. When he entered the hut it was quite dark there. He at once detected a sort of smell which recalled a hospital. He distinguished two groups of people. One of these comprised the doctor and Nadiéshda Alecsiċëvna, who were standing near a high bed. Under the sheepskin cover lay an elderly woman with her head thrown back and her eyes closed. The doctor was looking at a thermometer. The deacon screwed up his eyes trying to distinguish Cyril, but did not find him. He then looked at the other group. On a low bed near the stove lay a boy about ten years old covered with a woman's jacket. Cyril was holding him by the hand. The deacon went up to him. He was frightened when he looked at his son and saw how thin and pale his face had become. Cyril looked as if he ought to be numbered among the patients.

"Cyril!" quietly said the old man to his son, almost into his ear; and when Cyril lifted up his eyes the deacon shook his head. Cyril dropped the sick boy's hand and got up. He kissed his father.

"You see, bátoushka, what a state we are in!—terrible!" said he, turning round to the doctor and to Madame Kroupiéëv; and added—"This is my father; a most excellent old man."

The doctor got up and shook hands with the deacon. Nadiéshda Alecsiċëvna, lifted up her head and looked steadily at him, as though trying to distinguish his character.

"Let us come outside for a moment," said the deacon to Cyril.

Cyril took up his hat and they went together into the courtyard.

"You see I have not come alone. Your mother-in-law is also here; . . . she is very angry, and your wife is also vexed."

"And you?" asked Cyril—"are you vexed?"

"That's not exactly the question. Anna Nikoláevna wishes to take away your wife and child."

Cyril thought for a moment, as though reflecting whether this was a good thing or not. He then said—

"It will be well for them to go. They will find things better there. Everything here is upset and uncomfortable. When it is ended, Mura will come back."

"And won't you be dull, Cyril?"

"No," firmly answered he, "I shall not."

The deacon sat down on an earth mound, and Cyril returned into the hut. The old man gave up all thoughts of influencing his son. The tone in which Cyril spoke quite put a stop to all hopes. It was evident that he was so thoroughly absorbed by his work that no circumstances, no personal losses of the gravest nature could deter him from the business to which he had given up his whole existence. Strangely enough, up to that time he had been agitated, but directly he had seen his son he became quite calm, as though convinced by his motionless face and calm speech.

Absorbed by his thoughts, the deacon suddenly looked up and saw an old man sitting near him on the mound. He looked at his neighbour. He was a very old man, quite grey, with a wrinkled face, with dim and faded eyes. He was weeping, and he wiped his eyes with his fists.

"Eh, old man! why do you cry? God is merciful!" said the deacon, wishing to console him.

"It's not about that! it's not about that!" muttered the old man, in a trembling voice, evidently not noticing who he was addressing. "It's from joy that I cry—from joy!"

"And what is there to rejoice about?"

"Christ-like people have appeared on the earth—that's it! They are like saints. For example, the bátoushka: he is young, but what noble things he has done! . . . Ah!—ah!—ah! I have lived eighty years on the earth, my friend, and never saw the like. Truly he is sent by Divine Providence! . . . And then the lady and the doctor, how they have worked. . . . They are angels, and not people! . . . Real angels. And you know, my friend, when we see such people it makes us feel ashamed to sin. . . . Angels! angels!"

The old man crossed himself and wept. The deacon was much touched and hardly restrained his tears.

When he and Cyril returned together to the church-house, they found everything empty. Cyril went into the bedroom and looked at the chest of drawers: it was empty, and all Mura's belongings had disappeared from it. He looked at the baby's bed, on which lay the bare mattress, and a certain unpleasant feeling of loneliness seized him. "To go without even saying good-bye," and he mentally reproached Mura; "how distant we are from one another!"

He said little to his father. The deacon induced him to go to bed early. He was very anxious about his son's health as he noticed his glowing eyes and parched lips.

"You are too good to live—too good!" sadly thought the old man, sitting by his son's bedside long after midnight.

He also wondered to himself whence his son had derived such an enthusiastic spirit. His mother was an irritable woman, and he himself a shy, retiring man. Nazar also was a man of quite a different type, and Mefódii, although only in the third class, was already thinking about how he could secure a good place.

"Who do you take after?" asked the deacon, not taking his eyes off Cyril. But Cyril was sleeping soundly after forty-eight hours of watching and work.

XV.

IT was a gloomy day. The chime of the parish church bells echoed through the village with unusual solemnity. The church was filled to overflowing, and even the space outside the doors was crowded with people. There were as many people there as on the night of Easter eve. After a sorrowful week, Sunday had come. By this time people's minds had already become easier. Dr. Sapóshkof's skill, Madame Kroupiéëv's devotion and liberality, Cyril's energy in urging on an "impromptu" band of volunteers, had all helped to improve the state of things. Cyril officiated at the mass. Never before had the parishioners seen him as he was now. He had become terribly thin, his cheeks were sunken, and, arrayed in his priestly robes, he seemed to them nobler than he had ever been. Worn out by the fatigues of the past week, he walked slowly, and pronounced the prayers impressively, thoughtfully uttering each word. His voice was low, but the stillness in the church was so great, and the congregation so attentive, that every word was clearly heard.

Nadiéshda Alecsiéëvna was in church. She also looked thinner than usual. By her side stood her dark-eyed boy, gazing with astonishment at the church, and all that was going on around him. Madame Kroupiéëv had never before taken him to church. But she specially wished that he should see on that day how Cyril officiated, and how the people prayed. The deacon Obnovliénski, stood near Dementii in the choir. Not far from the choir stood Dr. Sapóshkof, who considered his mission as ended, and was returning the same day to the town.

The mass ended, and the people went out of church, but they did not disperse as usual, but remained outside the building. The crowd was so dense that it was impossible to move. It was evident that they were awaiting something. After a few minutes the church was quite empty. Only Madame Kroupiéëv and the doctor waited for Cyril to come out of the vestry, as she had invited him to the manor-house to *déjeuner*. The clerk's wife had also received an invitation, but as she was a lady of very shy and retiring disposition, she had not joined the others, and had remained standing in an obscure corner of the church. Father Simeon and Dementii bustled about near the altar, and the old deacon waited in the choir. At length Cyril appeared from behind the eikonostasis, and shook hands with Madame Kroupiéëv and the doctor. Cyril's father joined them, the clerk's wife came out from her obscure corner, and they all moved off towards the door.

Cyril went first. As soon as he appeared in the porch, simultaneously, several hundred heads were uncovered, and an indistinct murmur was heard in the crowd, followed by perfect silence. Cyril stopped, surprised by this unexpected sight, and the others behind him also stood where they were.

There was a movement in the crowd, and a tall, thin, dried-up old man, with a thin white beard, small eyes, and a small bald head, came out from among the people. He stopped and leant with his hands crossed on a thick stick.

"Bátoushka," said he, in a trembling, but in a loud and distinct voice, and with his head shaking—"Bátoushka, and you ladies and gentlemen! The Lord has visited us, but on account of our poverty we cannot repay you for your services. But what our feelings are— let the whole village commune say what we feel! I will only say, that such bátoushkas and such ladies and gentlemen never were before seen on the earth, and never will be again. That's what we feel!"

The old man lifted up his arm and wiped his fast-flowing tears with the worn-out sleeve of his coat.

At this moment a still more unexpected event occurred. The old man knelt down and made a profound bow to the ground. Many others followed his example. Others re-echoed his words of gratitude, and the mingled sound of their voices made a sort of indistinct murmur. Several women, overcome by emotion, ran up to the porch, seized the end of Cyril's cassock and pressed it to their lips. Tears were in nearly all eyes. Nadiéshda Alecsiéëvna, overcome by this touching scene, leant against a small column, fearing that her legs would no longer support her. This was too much for her unstrung nerves. Cyril, on the other hand, felt a surprising flow of energy and manfulness. At this moment he felt that a strong, unbreakable bond had been cemented between him and his parishioners, and that now he had a far greater influence than formerly over these people. He felt that all the words he had said to them before, had probably had but little effect, that if he now repeated his advice it would make an irresistible impression on their minds. He had to reply to the old man's speech, so, lifting up his hand with that same majestic motion which he made when appealing for help to Madame Kroupiéëv, he said—

"Listen to me, my friends! God has visited you for your sins, but who among us can say that he will not sin again in the future, and thus incur another visitation? Such a calamity may occur again, and find you unprepared for it. So listen to me, now that your hearts are purified by affliction: swear that you will never drink more than you ought, and that the money which you would have spent in this *vodka*, will be put into a common fund for mutual assistance, against an evil day."

"We will!" answered voices from the crowd. "We will close the publichouse, and make an agreement."[1]

"No, no!" replied Cyril. "An agree-

---

[1] The system of local option prevails in Russian villages. The "mir," or village commune, has the right to grant a license for a public-house, and to withdraw it. They generally receive a sum of money from the proprietor for the concession. This agreement would be a formal act, closing the public-house.

ment may always be broken. Close the public-house, and you will then have to go thirty versts for *vodka;* no agreements are required. You give me your promise now, on the spot. Do you promise?

"We promise!" thundered the crowd, like one man.

As soon as Cyril had descended the steps leading to the porch, he found himself in some one's embrace. This proved to be the old man who had made the speech. The embraces went on without end, and extended to the doctor and Madame Kroupiéëv and the old deacon, who was most affected of all.

Nadiéshda Alecsiéëvna scarcely managed to get into her carriage, the various impressions of the last half hour had quite unnerved her.

When her guests, who had undergone the process of being hugged by nearly all the villagers, arrived at the manor-house, she was scarcely in a state to receive them. Cyril, on the other hand, was very lively, cheerful, and talked a great deal. He triumphantly reflected that he would in future work among his flock under quite altered circumstances. An indissoluble bond was now established between him and his parishioners, and in one week he had gained an extraordinary influence over them. He spoke about the complete extermination of drunkenness, about establishing a reserve fund, which would enable them to improve their farming operations, about starting schools for grown-up people.

"Ah, yes, Nadiéshda Alecsiéëvna, we have got firm ground under our feet now. We have conquered Lúgovoë to-day, and now, with your help, we can do a deal of good work," said he.

Nadiéshda Alecsiéëvna smiled in a melancholy way, and her eyes looked at him inquiringly and sadly. During *déjeuner* she hardly ate anything, and took little part in the conversation. Directly after the meal was ended, a *taratáika* came round for the doctor and for Cyril's father, who had decided to go to the town to find out the state of the situation with regard to the Fortificantofs.

"Ah! how sorry I am to say good-bye to you dear, sympathetic people! Awfully sorry!" said Sapóshkof, seating himself on an improvised cushion of hay in the *taratáika*. "By the way, bátoushka, don't forget to look after that woman—what's her name?—Perepitchka; you must change her compress," added he.

The deacon silently kissed Cyril, and said—" You must think about yourself a bit, my son; neither God nor your conscience forbid this."

Cyril asked to be remembered to all the family, and to tell Mura that things were now better in Lúgovoë, and that she and Gavroushka could return. The clerk's wife also took her leave, perfectly satisfied with her reward for her labours at having been admitted into such brilliant society.

Nadiéshda Alecsiéëvna and Cyril were left alone.

"Let us come into the garden," said she; "I want some fresh air!" They went out together. The sun was obscured by grey, motionless clouds, like a thickening mist, but without any promise of rain. A faint breeze just stirred the branches of the trees. Here and there on the ground lay dried-up fallen leaves. The air was filled with a pleasant freshness.

They walked together. The little boy ran on in front. Every nook and corner of the garden was familiar to him as he had passed his whole life in the house and the garden. The boy was a sort of well-educated savage who had scarcely seen any people, and looked upon every one besides his mother and the chief bailiff as strangers. The last few weeks, however, he had become accustomed to Cyril and used to call him " my man."

· Nadiéshda Alecsiéëvna threw a white shawl over her shoulders, and every now and then, shuddering, wrapped it closer round herself.

" You are not well, Nadiéshda Alecsiéëvna!" said Cyril, looking at her pale and exhausted face.

She smiled bitterly, nervously shrugged her shoulders, and pulled her shawl closer round her body.

" Yes, I have broken down; it is time for me to retire from active service," and she gave a short and constrained laugh. Cyril thought, " She is not well," and answered nothing.

" Why don't you answer?" continued Madame Kroupiéëv; " why don't you say—' What! you are such a young hand to retire already: you have scarcely finished one small work, and you want to give up!' Why don't you say this to me? Give me your arm—I feel as if I shall fall.

Cyril was not in the habit of giving his arm to ladies, and it seemed to him as if the long sleeves of his cassock would rather interfere with the operation. But Madame Kroupiéëv, approaching him, took his arm herself, and firmly leant on it.

"You require a rest, Nadiéshda Alecsiéëvna," said Cyril. Madame Kroupiéëv paid no attention to this remark.

"I have lived a stupid life," said she, in a quiet voice, as though with the intention that he alone should hear her; "in my whole life there has only been one important fact, and that was the greatest folly which I have committed. . . . The people I have met with have always inspired me with contempt. . . . You are the only man whom I honour!"

Cyril felt that she was trembling, and that her quiet voice might at any moment be changed into weeping.

"We will work together now," said he, quietly.

"Look here," continued she, in the same quiet voice—"why do you wear that cassock? You don't really believe. . . . Take it off!"

In her quiet, scarcely audible voice something in the nature of a demand was heard.

"Who told you that? I believe in God, who has helped me to reach the hearts of these dark people. Without that I should never have done what I have," answered Cyril, in a tone of firm conviction.

"Very well! But why do you wear that cassock?"

"Why? Why in order to have the

right to go amongst them in their everyday life."

"Ah!" murmured she, in a painful tone; "these are words, mere words! Why are you to give up all for them? Am I not a poor creature, as worthy of compassion as they? Have we not also the right to a portion of happiness? And I want happiness. . . . Listen!"

As though struck by a sudden blow, he suddenly dropped her arm, stepped back a little, and looked at her with an astonished expression.

"You . . . you?" said he, feeling that his tongue would not act, and that he was unable to express himself.

Nadiéshda Alecsiéëvna approached the trunk of an apple-tree, the branches of which hung over their heads, and put out her arm and leant against it. She did not look at Cyril. Her face looked darker than usual in the grey atmosphere, and seemed to express a complete collapse of spirit, and interminable grief. She continued speaking in the same low tone which gave the impression that she might burst into tears at any moment.

"Yes, you are guilty in this matter. Why did you come to me with your uprightness, which I had never met with before in other people, with your deep sincerity, the existence of which I had never before believed in? You stirred me out of my dreamy listlessness, which at any rate never bred in me any questionings, desires, or demands. I was living as though half asleep, and you aroused me. One inspired look from you electrified me, and I followed you without asking whither or why;

and when I have reached such a condition that I cannot do without you, that I am ready to become your humble slave and to follow you everywhere, you look at me with surprise. Why? This is not just; this is the first time you are not sincere with me! You ought to sympathize with me—this is so natural—we have so much in common, and we understand one another so well!"

"And all this you say to me, a clergyman with a wife!" at length rejoined he.

"You do not love your wife—you cannot love her. Do not tell me such an untruth!" she answered, sharply. Her voice fell again, and became weaker than before: "Forgive me, and forget all that I have said to you. . . . I have made a mistake. . . . I shall leave here to-day!"

She quickly walked away down the path, then turned to the left and was lost to sight behind thick bushes. Cyril remained motionless for several seconds. His first impulse was to follow her: it seemed to him that she walked so feebly, that she required support. But then he thought that such assistance would only make matters worse. He turned back. He felt conscious that she was crying, but nevertheless he directed his steps towards the gate. He feared to turn back, and thought with horror of the scene which had just passed, and which was for him perfectly unexpected.

He returned home with hasty steps, as though he feared pursuit. He now understood that look of liveliness which had appeared on Nadiéshda Alecsiéëvna's face when he visited her, and the readiness with which she followed him, and at a word from him opened her purse and her granaries to the moujiks who, up to that time, she had never noticed. He recalled also the looks she had cast at him when he was addressing the crowd that day near the church. All this, together with the unexpected conclusion which had just taken place, was altogether strange and incomprehensible to him. He was too simple. He could not understand the possibility of talking about love to a man who already had a wife and a child, especially when this man was a priest. It was evening when he reached home. The night air felt damp, and he was anxious to get into his house. Entering and passing through the rooms, he suddenly felt a sense of loneliness. He wanted to see Mura and his son, and a torturing chill crept over his heart.

For a long time he wandered about the house, the quiet of which was disturbed only by the sound of his own steps. This sound, which he had not before noticed, not having been alone, was particularly disagreeable to him. A thousand various thoughts and impressions sprang up in his mind, and he thought how hard it was to reconcile the various demands of different people with his life.

Feókla entered the room, carrying a lighted candle.

"Ah! bátoushka, there are two letters for you," said she.

Feókla looked at him furtively. She did not approve of his conduct, and could not forgive him for having let Mura go.

"Letters?" said Cyril, going towards her with sudden animation.

"Yes, one is lying there on the table. From the town, I suppose; the village policeman has just brought it. And here is another one, come this moment from the manor-house."

Cyril stretched out his hand; Feókla gave him a small note.

Inside the envelope was a visiting-card, on the back of which was written—"I beg you, as a friend, to forget all that has passed to-day between us, and only to preserve a kindly recollection of me. I am leaving here at once. When *I am recovered*, I will return and help you, but now I can be of no use. I have made arrangements that the people shall continue to receive help from me. What a noble and pure soul you have!"

Cyril slowly tore up the card and threw the pieces into the waste-paper basket. He saw before him Nadiéshda Alecsićëvna's pale face, brilliant eyes, and heaving breast, when she was addressing those strange words to him. And he suddenly felt pity for her, as for a sick person, and regretted that it was not in his power to shake hands with her once more and take leave of her. And after all, she had spent her money, her time, and her strength nobly.

"Yes, it is merely an illness; it will pass away, and Nadiéshda Alecsićëvna will return, and we shall meet as friends," thought he.

He then suddenly remembered about the other letter. The envelope was addressed in Anna Nikoláevna's handwriting.

"Ah! it's not from Mura," thought he, opening the letter.

The dignitary's wife wrote laconically, but majestically—"My dear Son-in-law, Cyril Ignatievitch,—Your mad doings have driven us almost out of our wits, and we were compelled to take from you your wife, our daughter, together with our grandson. We imagined, naturally enough, that the following day you would fly to the town to your family, but we were mistaken—the idea even does not seem to have occurred to you. Your wife is weeping, but is too proud to return to you. You will only find yourself again in your family when you have come to your senses. Wishing you and my daughter every happiness, I remain your mother-in-law, ANNA FORTIFICANTOF. P.S.—The bishop is willing to appoint you to a place in the merchants' church, if you wish it."

Cyril folded up the letter and replaced it on the table. He walked twice up and down the room, then stopped opposite the window and looked out on the village. In the thickening shades of evening, the peasants' huts looked like indistinct patches; here and there lights were visible. He felt that for the sake of personal happiness, for the sake of a peaceful and plentiful life, he would abandon this grey village and settle in the town in the rich parish of the merchants' church. But immediately this idea seemed to him absurd and unfeasible.

"To come to one's senses! That means to enter on the well-trodden path, to live without aims in life, without ideas! No, I will never come to my senses! Never!

Let me then live alone—let them even deprive me of my son!"

But then he felt that his son was necessary to him, and that sooner or later he would claim him. He would teach his son how he must live; on this point he would never yield. He would instil his own ardent spirit into him, and make him a man like himself. And, after all, was he alone? These grey huts, under whose roofs so many important lives were passing—was he not necessary to them? Had he not conquered them, and made himself dear to them? Cyril remembered the sick woman the doctor had spoken to him about. He put on his cassock, took his stick, and with a firm step descended into the street.

www.ingramcontent.com/pod-product-compliance
Lightning Source LLC
Chambersburg PA
CBHW021840230426
43669CB00008B/1031